CLAIM YOUR FREE 30 SECOND PRESENTATION MASTER

Simply complete this coupon and send it to us to receive your free guide to perfect presentation. Packed with tips and practical suggestions the 30 SECOND PRESENTATION MASTER helps you make first-class presentations every time.

☐ *I would like to receive further information on the Ready Made Activities Resource Packs*

Name: _____ Position: _____

Company/Organisation: _____

Address (including postcode): _____

_____

Country: _____

Telephone: _____ Fax: _____

Nature of business: _____

Title of book purchased: _____

Comments: _____

_____

GW00507932

---------------------- **Fold Here Then Staple** ----------------------

We would be very grateful if you could answer these questions to help us with market research.

1 Where/How did you hear of this book?
☐ in a bookshop
☐ in a magazine/newspaper
(please state which):

_____

☐ information through the post
☐ recommendation from a colleague
☐ other (please state which):

_____

2 Which newspaper(s)/magazine(s) do you read regularly?:

_____

_____

3 When buying a business book which factors influence you most?
(Please rank in order)
☐ recommendation from a colleague
☐ price
☐ content
☐ recommendation in a bookshop
☐ author
☐ publisher
☐ title
☐ other(s):

4 Is this book a
☐ personal purchase?
☐ company purchase?

5 Would you be prepared to spend a few minutes talking to our customer services staff to help with product development? YES/NO

Ready made activities for
FINANCIAL SKILLS

Ready made activities for FINANCIAL SKILLS

Derrick Fellows

the Institute of Management

FOUNDATION

PITMAN PUBLISHING

PITMAN PUBLISHING
128 Long Acre, London WC2E 9AN

A Division of Longman Group Limited

First published in Great Britain 1994

© Derrick Fellows 1994

British Library Cataloguing in Publication Data
A CIP catalogue record for this book can be obtained from the British Library.

ISBN 0 273 60730 8

10 9 8 7 6 5 4 3 2 1

Typeset by PanTek Arts, Maidstone, Kent.
Printed and bound in England by Clays Ltd, St Ives plc

It is the Publishers' policy to use paper manufactured from sustainable forests.

Contents

About the author   vi

Acknowledgement   vii

Part 1 Introduction   1

Help is at hand   3

How to use this book   5

Tips for the trainer   7

Part 2 The Activities   11

Session 1   What's it all about?   13

Session 2   Where the figures come from and go to   19

Session 3   Have we done well?   44

Session 4   Where are we now?   58

Session 5   Do we understand what's going on?   83

Session 6   Where do we go from here?   125

Session 7   So what *is* the bottom line?   159

About the author

Derrick Fellows is a management training consultant, having established his business in 1982 and operated it continuously ever since. He has studied extensively and holds a number of professional qualifications. He is a Fellow of the Institutes of Company Accountants, Financial Accountants and Personnel and Development, a Member of the Association of Business Executives and of Mensa and an Associate of the Institute of Chartered Secretaries and Administrators.

Although his main activity is management training (including finance for non-financial managers), he has always done his own accounts. This provides him with the ability and experience to approach this subject simultaneously from the viewpoints of a trainer, a practitioner and a qualified company secretary. His Finance for Non-Financial Managers course is listed by OMTRAC as one of the best in the United Kingdom.

He is available to provide the training described in this book.

Acknowledgement

I would like to express my deepest appreciation to Susan Kaer for her patience and application in wading through my draft for this book. Apart from checking for mistakes in the text and figures, as an experienced trainer with a limited knowledge of finance her consideration of the book as a learning medium for herself and as a tool for training others was of great value.

1

....

INTRODUCTION

Help is at hand!

I hope this book will prove valuable to you and flexible enough to meet your own needs, whatever they may be. Should you like the contents and wish to train people on finance the material should be sufficient to run a three-day course. If you prefer, however, I can conduct a course for you on an 'in-house' basis for between one and nine participants or, alternatively, I provide 'open' courses on a regular basis so that you can send people to me for training.

Apart from Finance for Non-Financial Managers, I also provide 'open' courses on the following subjects:

Instructional Techniques
Inter-Personal Skills, Leadership and the Manager
Problem Solving and Decision Making
Interviewing Skills for Selection and Appraisal
Effective Presentation
Planning and Organising
Handling Conflict
Improving the Effectiveness of Teams

As well as providing the above 'open' courses, I can tailor them to your needs and conduct them on an 'in-house' basis as required. Other in-house courses which I have designed and conducted for a wide variety of clients over the years are:

Effective Group Training
Positive Management Through Persuasion
Managing People Effectively
Selection Interviewing
Appraisal Interviewing
Quality Through Problem Solving
Motivation, Delegation and Management
Motivation, Delegation and Leadership
Leadership in Action
Leadership Through Persuasion
Synergistic Decision Making

Effective Discipline
Effective Letter Writing
Management Skills and Self-Development
Improving Clerical Efficiency
Planning Profits Through People
Leadership and Team Development
Organisation Development Through Performance Improvement Planning
Developing the Senior Administrator

If you would like me to provide training for you, you can contact me as follows:

Derrick Fellows,
Consultancy and Training Services,
63, Wynndale Road,
Woodford,
London, E18 1DY
United Kingdom

Telephone: 0181-504 4639

I will gladly send you a brochure on request. Happy training!

How to use this book

I have written this book from the starting point of providing ready-made material for the reader to use in conducting training in finance for non-financial people. To this end, I have started from the basics and gradually built up a broad outline of the subject in order that people will *understand* the figures they are using. My aim is that they will know where the figures came from, how they got to wherever they are, what their significance and limitations are and how they can best be used to improve analysis, decision making and planning.

I have not attempted to cover taxation in the book. People are sometimes curious about taxation, but it is far too complicated a subject to include and the rules applying are frequently changed. It is most unlikely that company taxation would form an essential part of a line manager's knowledge; where such information is required, I would strongly advise an approach to a tax expert!

I have used a working example throughout the book; this can be used by the person conducting the training for their presentation. I have written the text in a way which speaks to the reader as a trainer, so that they will be able to present information, ask questions, anticipate answers and give explanations. At the end of the presentation section of each chapter, I have summarised the key learning points. Apart from Chapter 1, I have then provided a range of exercises which the trainer can use in practice sessions. It is my experience (particularly with this subject) that it is only when people are asked to *do* something in the light of what has been covered that you (and they) find out whether they *really* understand it or not!

There is sufficient material in each chapter to prepare OHP slides in advance as well as suggestions for using the flip-chart.

Although I have approached this book with the trainer in mind, it could be a useful and flexible learning resource for anyone wanting to develop an understanding of finance for themselves. I have assumed that I am teaching the trainer as well as the trainee, so once the reader gets used to being 'talked to' as a trainer in the book they could use it purely as a learning tool in its own right.

Many textbooks on finance are very heavy going and often hard to follow. I hope this is not the case with mine and that anyone studying finance on a course would also find this book very helpful and practical. The exercises will be particularly useful once an understanding of the material in each chapter is in place and they could also be used separately as a resource.

I have found it extremely useful when running training courses on this subject to have access to a wide range and quantity of prepared 'extra' exercises which I can pull out and use with some or all of the trainees as each session progresses. It may not be essential to use all of the exercises or to give them to every trainee on a course. Usually, there are one or two trainees who complete a given exercise in half the time needed by the others – it is good to have the option of keeping them challenged and reinforcing their learning by having additional, ready-made materials to hand. I would also mention that the exercises are very flexible in another way, in that they can be completed individually, in syndicates or plenary session. They may also be used as 'homework'!

I have found it particularly helpful when conducting a course on such a technical subject to add a little variety with the way I use exercises. On a three-day course, it can prove very stimulating for everyone to have one or two challenging exercises on the third day completed by the whole group as a team, where it is everyone's responsibility to ensure that *they* understand and agree the answers and how they are derived *and* that every other member of the team does too. This way, frustration and humour arise and it gives you the opportunity of using those who have grasped the subject more effectively to help those who have not. The trainer's role becomes much more of a controlling and facilitating one at this stage, which is a pleasant change for everyone. Finance is a very gruelling subject for most people, the trainer included (if for no other reason than for the degree of concentration and patience that is required).

I will now give a few tips which you may find useful when conducting training on finance; many are based on lots of experiences which have highlighted several likely pitfalls.

Tips for the trainer

1 Go *slowly*. No matter how slowly you think you are going, it is quite likely to be a little fast for most people.

2 Don't *assume* that people can operate a simple calculator. Calculators work differently from one another and may produce different answers when used the same way! It is vital that each participant fully understands their own calculator and can use the memory and percentage calculations as well as addition, subtraction, multiplication and division – nothing more than these functions will be needed for the content of this book.

3 Make absolutely certain that YOU fully understand and are comfortable with all the book's content *before* attempting to use it for training others! Make sure all the figures work for you and that you know where they come from and why I've used them.

4 Given the opportunity and the inclination, prepare additional exercises and examples which will add to those in the book – you never know when you might need them and it is very difficult to invent figures which work 'on the spot'.

5 You are likely to be asked questions which you can't answer, or which could side-track you; don't be frightened to admit that you don't know the answer (for example, a question on taxation – which is an even more complicated subject in its own right). If a 'detour' is threatened, follow it as long as you have time and it maintains everybody's interest!

6 Listen to questions very carefully; terms and descriptions are often misused or imprecise (e.g. 'profit'). Try to answer the question as asked, clarify it by asking a question back (e.g. 'what *type* of profit?'), point out that when trainees ask questions on financial issues they need to be precise and really understand the terms they choose to use. Try very hard to phrase *your* questions in a very precise way.

7 Encourage people to use logic to address financial questions, rather than simply picking and using a formula. I make this point in the text, because people often don't recognise answers as wrong if they simply use formulae. They also end up being able to deal with financial information only

when it is presented in *exactly* the same format which you used to teach them (and, of course, figures and terminology are so diverse that formats will always vary in practice).

8 Be patient, clear and precise. Don't jump in too quickly with answers to questions or exercises which you have presented – give them every chance to work things out for themselves. There is a very fine balance here – sometimes people get annoyed if they feel that you are not helping them enough.

9 Finance can be a very dry subject. It is intricate and requires a good deal of concentration by everyone concerned. People will regress and no longer understand things which they had grasped a few hours before! It is very important, therefore, to add variety and colour at every opportunity. Use the flip-chart and the OHP, allow and encourage questions and discussions from/with the trainees, use exercises in different ways, ask them questions at regular intervals to assess, summarise and reinforce what you have covered and (where time permits and as people become more proficient) take time to look at any financial documents which the trainees have brought with them (or the organisation's annual report if available).

10 Ask or encourage trainees to go over what they have learned in the evenings. Exercises can be done overnight, but it is more important that people consolidate and reinforce what they learned by re-studying what you have covered.

11 Encourage people to take notes. At the end of the training, give a copy of this book to each person for further study of and reference to what they have learned.

Many of these points apply to training in relation to other subjects, but they are never more important than when teaching finance.

As a guide, I would suggest the following outline for a three-day course based on this book (be warned, however, that people may take less, or a good deal more, time to assimilate the information and complete the exercises, depending on their abilities and frame of mind at the time).

Exercises may be left out or put in at different times according to how things go during a given session. On these timings, Exercises G and H are held back but could be used in place of (or as well as) some of those suggested, or to extend the training period. The overnight exercises can, of course, also be interchanged for maximum flexibility. As I emphasised earlier, any additional exercises which you can design might also be worth having as extra material.

Chapter/Exercise	Duration (mins)	Day	Timings
Introduction	30	1	0900–0930
SESSION 1	60	1	0930–1030
Coffee	15	1	1030–1045
SESSION 2	90	1	1045–1215
Exercise A	30	1	1215–1245
Lunch	60	1	1245–1345
SESSION 3	60	1	1345–1445
Exercise B	20	1	1445–1505
Tea	15	1	1505–1520
SESSION 4	60	1	1520–1620
Exercise C	20	1	1620–1640
Exercise D	45	1	Overnight
Exercise E	45	2	0900–0945
SESSION 5	45	2	0945–1030
Coffee	15	2	1030–1045
SESSION 5 (continued)	60	2	1045–1145
Exercise F	60	2	1145–1245
Lunch	60	2	1245–1345
Exercise I	60	2	1345–1445
SESSION 6	20	2	1445–1505
Tea	15	2	1505–1520
SESSION 6 (continued)	45	2	1520–1605
Exercise J	45	2	1605–1650
Exercise K	55	2	Overnight
Exercise L	30	3	0900–0930
SESSION 7	60	3	0930–1030
Coffee	15	3	1030–1045
SESSION 7 (continued)	30	3	1045–1115
Exercise M	30	3	1115–1145
Exercise N	30	3	1145–1215
Exercise O	15	3	1215–1230
Exercise P	15	3	1230–1245
Lunch	60	3	1245–1345
Exercise Q	70	3	1345–1455
Tea	15	3	1455–1510
Exercise R	30	3	1510–1540
Exercise S	45	3	1540–1625
Evaluation	20	3	1625–1645

2

THE ACTIVITIES

Session 1

· ·

What's it all about?

Divide the group into small syndicates of three or four people for 15 minutes; ask each syndicate to discuss

What is finance and why is it important?

To stimulate and enlarge discussions and ideas where necessary, you can inject as appropriate the thought that this can be from the viewpoint of all interested parties (e.g. owners/managers/employees/competitors/customers/suppliers/potential investors/inland revenue).

Ask the syndicates to write their findings on a flip-chart and then have them report back to the main group.

As an alternative you could hold this discussion with the whole group and list their responses on the flip-chart yourself. Some of the main points to be made are as follows:

- finance is an essential aspect of all organisations, whether profit-making or not
- before any organisation can do anything, it must have *some* resources which have a monetary value
- finance is therefore as vital at the start as is the product itself – more so, in fact
- finance is fundamentally concerned with sources of funding, how and where the funding is applied, and with the control of the funds
- whether we like it or not, finance is an unavoidable tool when reviewing and assessing the performance and position of any organisation
- finance affects *everyone* working in or interacting with the organisation.

Some of the specific functions of finance from the viewpoint of the interested parties (listed above) would include supplying information about the organisation's

- profitability
- future prospects
- solvency
- efficiency
- stability
- dividends
- capital growth value

- asset valuations
- share price valuation vs. real worth
- outstanding liabilities
- honesty
- credit-worthiness
- risk factors
- owners

Make the point that finance is the means of making an assessment of all these factors; without it, we would not know where to put our resources or whether past allocations were correct.

Summarise and list on the flip-chart or OHP the main functions of finance:

- to decide on the size and best allocations of resources
- to control the resources employed in an organisation
- to assess the success of asset allocation decisions
- to provide essential information to various interested parties (of whom there are many)
- to prevent dishonesty and inaccurate information.

Finance is therefore concerned with the provision of vital, accurate information for use by various interested decision-makers, rather than with wealth creation in its own right. Since all managers are decision-makers, every manager really should have a sound understanding of finance in order to understand the information which is available to them. Unfortunately, many managers accept tables of figures without knowing how they are drawn up, what they represent or how to use them. This places them at an immense disadvantage to other people who may have that understanding and means that the decisions they take are unlikely to be the best they could make. That is why *you* need to understand what is going on in financial terms.

While understanding finance can seem daunting and somewhat akin to learning a foreign language with mathematics thrown in, the knowledge and skills will give any manager a strong advantage at work. This is something which is generally lacking in this country and which should help you progress your career as the quality and justification of your future decisions improve the outcomes. An understanding of finance can also be of immense value *outside* work, since we are all faced with increasing financial demands, options and opportunities because of a widening array of financial products (mortgages,

PEPS, personal pensions, unit and investment trusts, investment bonds and so on).

Let's look at an example of what information an organisation might require in order to gather the financial data on which everything will eventually be based. Show the following list:

Costs	£
London to Rome	350
Expenses in Rome	450
Rome to Brussels	200
Expenses in Brussels	330
Brussels to London	250
Total	1,580

Someone undertakes the above business excursion. The list shows the costs involved. While they may think this suffices, the accountant will require a different breakdown of the expenses. Write the following list on the flip-chart:

Travel	800
Hotels and meals	550
Telephone calls and faxes	125
Gifts to potential customers	50
Meeting room hire	55
	1,580

Point out that the total expenses are the same – £1,580. The difference is because the underlying nature of each expense must be identified in order to record it in the appropriate individual account of the organisation. If the organisation does not do this, it will not be able to identify and assess the way in which it is allocating its resources and will therefore fail to enable 'finance' to do the job which we have highlighted above.

Make the point strongly that the *reason* people are asked to keep receipts and to complete expense forms is not merely to check their honesty (since a dishonest person could still 'fiddle' their expense claims without too much difficulty), but rather to enable the organisation to record the expenses in away which will be meaningful and helpful when assessing the performance of the business as a whole.

No two organisations are likely to use the same account classifications. For example, it might be important to a telesales company to have a separate account for telephone costs only, whereas a sole trader may include telephone costs along with things like stationery, postage and printing under one expense account called 'Administration Expenses'.

Taking our example above, let's suppose that the person making this excursion obtained orders worth £10,000; the goods supplied carry a margin of 25 per cent. Is this a worthwhile exercise? Use the response to demonstrate that the project will have made a profit of:

$$
\begin{array}{rl}
& £10,000 \\
- & £\ 7,500 \quad \text{(the cost of the products supplied)} \\
\hline
= & £\ 2,500 \quad \text{(the Gross Profit)} \\
- & £\ 1,580 \quad \text{(the costs of the exercise)} \\
\hline
= & £\quad 920 \quad \text{(the Net Profit for the project)}
\end{array}
$$

The question of whether the exercise was worthwile will depend on who is asking. To a manager of a multimillion pound empire, the answer may well be a definite 'NO!'. To a junior manager who likes going abroad, the answer may be the complete opposite (and, as we all know, self-interest does play a part!). On pure profit alone, a business which is currently making a loss might think the trip worthwhile, while many companies would assess it as not making a large enough profit.

Apart from *who* is asking, there may well be important additional information which we haven't taken into account – for instance, is office space in London still chargeable even though the occupier is away? Are later, repeat orders a possibility (where the actual trip abroad with its accompanying costs may not be necessary)? How much money was invested in the exercise, when will the return be received and could this investment have provided a greater return elsewhere? Are there dangers of bad debts, or currency fluctuations (where the value of the sales will be less in £ terms when received than originally envisaged).

What is significant? With financial information, it is a question which, can only be answered by the person who requires that information, based on *what* information they include! Significance, therefore, is a subjective thing.

State that a bookkeeper's role is to record and summarise all the financial events which occur in the organisation. Ask what the role of the accountant is. Discuss the suggestions to conclude that the accountant has several, much wider tasks, as follows:

1 To determine the classification of the accounts used. Point out that the individual expense accounts used depend on how the organisation is going to assess and use the information at the end of the year (or other period). It is no good incurring thousands of expense items and recording them in any old way; at the end of the year, it is too late (and too lengthy a process) to go back and redefine them under the headings required.

2 To determine what resources their department requires, in terms of people, equipment, space, powers and so on.

3 To manage the function/department/equipment/people.

4 To prepare and provide reports and reviews for a variety of purposes (e.g. annual accounts, budget documentation, financial reports as required).

5 An internal audit service to prevent mistakes and fraud.

6 To ensure the organisation meets statutory requirements with regard to the publication of financial accounts and the timely completion of government forms.

7 To determine tax liabilities in liaison with the Inland Revenue and Customs and Excise (and company policy).

All these tasks obviously depend on close association with the top management of the organisation, which is why there is usually a Finance Director on the Board. In fact, the Managing Director often comes from a financial background.This shows that an understanding of finance puts you at a great advantage, and may suggest that too many non-financial directors don't really understand what is going on in the business if they have failed to become financially literate. Something to bear in mind if you're still not convinced that an understanding of finance can enhance your own career prospects!

In fact, finance is based on a kind of scientific logic, although it might seem like the opposite to the uninitiated. This actually does make it interesting and not as difficult to learn as people might think. People fear what they don't understand – a normal human reaction. This has led to the misuse of finance by people who have avoided learning how to use it properly and who therefore make bad decisions and blame them on financial considerations.

This situation, combined with the disciplines imposed by using information sensibly and a few people who are actually dishonest and use their knowledge for personal gain, has created an unfair aura of dislike among many people. This is therefore an opportunity for *you* to learn how to take advantage of a useful subject, rather than having to be taken advantage of (by your colleagues/customers/suppliers/competitors and so on).

Let us end this session with two accounting conventions which are important. The first, known as **conservatism** (note the small 'c'!) means that a profit is never assumed, but a loss is allowed for. For this reason, we always value stocks at the lower of either **cost** (what we paid for them or what it cost us to manufacture them) or **market value**, for example.

The second convention you should be aware of is **consistency**. Much of finance is concerned with the comparison of information; such comparison would be worse than meaningless (it could be misleading) unless figures are calculated on a similar basis, with similar assumptions and valuations, from one period to the next or from one situation to another.

In conclusion of this session, I will summarise the following points:

- finance is a vital component of *all* organisations
- it provides *essential* information for assessment, decision-making and control purposes
- it is in *your* interest to understand finance
- meaningful classification of financial information is fundamentally important for its eventual usefulness
- the significance of financial information depends on *who* is using it, *what* they include and *why* they need it
- an accountant provides a vital management service
- accounting adopts the conventions of conservatism and consistency.

For your own benefit, remember:

- **every** manager needs the ability to exercise **control**
- finance underpins every facet of an organisation
- knowledge is power
- power gives control
- **you** therefore **need** this knowledge if you are to be in control.

Session 2

Where the figures come from and go to

Ask the group:

What is the first thing you should do when presented with a table of financial information?

Encourage suggestions (including humorous ones, such as 'throw it in the bin' or 'take a coffee break'). Whatever ideas materialise, make the following key point:

The first thing you should do is make absolutely sure that you understand where the figures came from and how they are worked out.

Explain to the group that any financial analysis, for whatever purpose, is dependent on the accumulation and effective presentation of data made up from numerous (probably thousands) of individual transactions. It is all very well to use a computer to produce summary information and analyses, but unless the human user fully understands where the figures came from and how they got to where they are now, there will be many dangers in reaching conclusions or taking decisions based on them.

Unfortunately, most people *don't* take this first step. When presented with figures, they tend to accept them as presented and try to use them *without really understanding what it is that they are looking at!* I am not suggesting that whoever prepared and presented the figures is falsifying the information, but simply that what the data actually portrays is *not* understood by anyone who hasn't seen *how* the figures were worked out. The terminology, mathematics, fear of looking a fool and peer pressure can all make it difficult for a manager to **ask** and **check** how the figures are worked out before trying to use them. The presence of 'an expert' at the meeting can easily lead to a tendency to leave the details to them, yet an 'expert' at figures may not be an expert in your area of work. It is also a common human failing to want to arrive at 'an answer' and difficult steps along the way may be skipped!

We are therefore going to take a careful look at how information is entered into the accounting system and how it is 'processed', so that later we will understand where all the information which we use for other purposes came from.

In the previous session, we talked about the need for, and importance of, **expense classification**. The basis of classification of expenses is largely dependent on the end requirements (how the information is to be summarised) of the particular organisation.

☞ *Ask*: what expense accounts can you think of?

List the responses on the flip-chart, possibly including:

motor expenses
printing and stationery
salaries and wages
advertising and display
lighting and heating
rent and business rates
legal expenses
research and development
telephone/faxes
depreciation

Note: cost of goods sold is not a separate account; if it were, it would be an expense account (but not an *operating* expense account). If it is suggested, add it on but mention that it is different to the others, as they will see later. Otherwise, don't mention it, as it might confuse people unnecessarily.

In fact, there are four types of account; all individual accounts may be allocated to one of these four categories. The first is (write in **blue** on the flip-chart 'Expense', then 'Sales' and go on to explain...):

Expense
Sales

Sales comprise all the revenue accounts, which could be made up of the individual accounts for each customer or, in a very small business, simply one account where there is no need to sub-divide.

 Note: write in **red** on the flip-chart (under the previous two items):

Assets

☞ *Ask:* what is an asset?

See if anyone can define the term and then agree/explain that an asset is something that has a residual value at the end of the year. This is quite different to an expense, which has no residual value and which has been used up *during* the year, e.g. wages have no remaining value once they have been paid and the work has been received.

☞ *Ask:* give me some examples of assets.

List the responses on a separate flip-chart page, possibly including:

motor vehicles
premises
fixtures and fittings
equipment
bank balance (if positive!)
cash
debtors
stocks
materials
work-in-progress

All these are assets and would almost certainly be listed in separate, individual accounts since the underlying items are very different in nature.

☞ *Ask:* what is the opposite of an asset?
Answer: a liability. Turn back to the previous page on the flip-chart and write in red (under the previous item, 'Assets'):

✎ Liabilities

This is the fourth type of account.

☞ *Ask:* what is a liability?

Ensure that everyone understands that a liability is an outstanding debt which will have to be paid by you at a later date. The most common liability is a trade creditor, but others might include unpaid tax or VAT, or a bank overdraft.

And now for a key point which often (but unnecessarily) causes confusion.

☞ *Ask:* what do we call someone to whom we owe money?
Answer: a **creditor**. A **debtor** is someone who owes us money! Stress that it is most important that people fully understand this point, since they often get it wrong and when they do it will really confuse them at a later time.

Another thing that people are likely to be confused by is the thought of a debtor as an **asset**; they may be more used to thinking of someone who owes them money as being a liability! Make sure they appreciate that a debtor *is* an asset and that the asset has a value. Proof of its value is that it can be 'sold on', or 'factored', to a third party who will pay you slightly less than is owed but collect the full amount themselves at a later time.

Key point: I have written these four types of account in two different colours for a reason. **Expenses** and **Sales** go together because they both end up being *transferred* to the Trading, Profit and Loss Account, as we shall see later. **Assets** and **Liabilities** are summarised separately in the Balance Sheet (which we shall also see later). The Balance Sheet is quite separate from the Trading, Profit and Loss Account and is *not* part of the double-entry system. It will help you a great deal from now on if you can distinguish between these two sets of two types of account, remembering which go where!

Note: make sure people have time to assimilate this important point. You will almost certainly need to refer back to these four types of account several times in future sessions to remind people and clarify the difference between the two pairs.

We are now going to look at the method of recording financial transactions in the accounts so that you understand where figures come from later. The system which is almost universally used is called 'double-entry book-keeping'. It is an extremely logical way of working, once you understand some basic ground-rules and concepts.

The term 'double-entry' derives from the fact that each financial transaction is recorded twice in the accounts. The logic to this is that

any transaction involves an exchange (of equal value) between two parties.

Each party is an entity in its own right and could be an individual, a partnership, a limited company, a charity, a social club or even a separate 'cost centre' within an organisation for accounting purposes. When viewed through the eyes of one of the entities involved in the transaction:

something of value is coming into the entity (for simplicity we shall assume that the entity is a company) and **something of equal value is going out.**

There are, therefore, two elements to every transaction, and *both* must be entered in the relevant accounts.

1 **Whatever is coming in to the entity is** *debited* **in the appropriate account**

2 **Whatever is going out (in exchange) is** *credited* **to a different account**

Make sure that everyone understands these concepts, before carrying on to the next point: **each individual account, of whatever type, has two sides – a** *credit* **side and a** *debit* **side.**

In each account, the left-hand side is for debit entries, while credit entries are made on the right-hand side.

Ask: when you pay money into your bank account (as an individual), how is the transaction recorded on your bank statement?

People invariably answer, 'It is credited'. Yet I have just told you that whatever is *coming in* is debited! How can this be so?

Note: this single point is crucial, since it is the basic reason why most people get credit and debit the wrong way round. Once they understand this point, things start to fall into place!

Usually, someone will suggest the reason this happens. Basically, it is because each transaction is from the viewpoint of one particular entity – in this case, through the bank's eyes. To the bank, money is coming in and would be debited in its *own* bank account. However, it has to make a credit entry to show *what is going out of the bank* – in this case, the **liability** to repay your money on demand. It therefore makes a corresponding credit entry of equal value in your account.

When the bank sends you a statement, it is *the bank's statement* of *your* account, not your's. To the bank, *you* are a **creditor** and your account is therefore a **liability** account!

If you were recording the same transaction in your own accounts, you would debit *your* bank account (while making a corresponding credit entry for whatever you had given in exchange for the money).

The crucial reason your bank statement shows a credit entry for money which you have paid in, therefore, is that the statement is a picture of the situation as seen from the bank. It is, in fact, the bank's statement, *not* yours (although we normally refer to it as 'our bank statement'!).

It can therefore be seen that the entries made by one of the two entities involved will be the opposite way around to the entries made by the other entity in its own accounts!

Make certain that this point is clearly understood, then re-emphasise the point that, when we are looking at any transaction through *our* eyes,

whatever is coming in is *debited* in the appropriate account

whatever is going out (in exchange) is *credited* to a different account.

And so, when we pay money into our bank account, we will make a debit entry in that account in *our* accounts, and know that it will be shown as a credit entry on the bank's statement when we receive it.

Now, let's look at some transactions and see how we would enter each one in the relevant accounts:

Date
(day and month)   *Transaction*

2.1   Issued £100,000 shares in one instalment

 Ask: what is coming into the business?
Answer: money/cheque/cash.
 Ask: where will we (the business) pay this money?
Answer: into the bank.

So let's open a bank account (write entries on the flip-chart, step by step, from now on, and point out that the 'DR' and 'CR' headings apply for all the accounts which follow).

	DR	CR
	Bank Account	
2.1 Share issue –	100,000	

Note: make quite sure you leave plenty of space between each account that you open. You will be making further entries later and will need to use two or three flip-chart pages for these accounts.

We have written the date of the transaction, the nature of it and the amount. But we have only made one entry.

 Ask: what is going out of the business?
Answer: (they may need help here): the (long-term) liability to repay the money to the owners. The business does not *own* anything and so money subscribed by the owners has to be repaid by the company at a later date. This liability is a form of debt owed by the company. The IOU is in the form of the share certificates, which have been sent *out* of the business to the owners. Therefore, we must now **credit** an account to show this liability – it is logical to name it Share Capital.

Share Capital Account	
2.1. Share issue – B.	100,000

Make the point that even where the business is a sole trader, transactions like this one would be viewed through the eyes of the business – even though, in reality, the owner *is* the business. From an accounting point of view, *the owner and the business are ALWAYS two separate entities!*

You may notice that we have again put in the date, nature of the transaction and the amount. This time, however, we have also indicated the name of the account where the other half of the double entry was made. What we need to include in our Bank Account entry, therefore, is the name of the Share Capital Account, thus:

Bank Account

2.1 Share Issue – Share Ca. 100,000

The reason for indicating where the other part of the double entry may be found is so that we can easily trace back what we have done should an error appear later. This would be an arduous task – searching among thousands of entries in numerous accounts – without such a facility. It is also helpful for the auditor or other authorised person who may be checking through the accounts.

The second transaction is:

3.1 Purchased premises for £50,000

Ask: what's going out of the business?
Answer: £50,000 from the bank. So this time we'll **credit** the Bank Account.
Ask: what's coming in?
Answer: the premises. So, we'll also open a Premises Account and make a debit entry there.

Bank Account

2.1 Share Issue – Share Ca. 100,000   3.1 Purchase – Premises 50,000

Premises Account

3.1 Purchase – Bank   50,000

Let's look at a third transaction:

3.1 Purchased equipment with cash for £10,000

Ask: where will my credit and debit entries go?
Answer: credit the Bank Account, open an Equipment Account and debit that.

Bank Account

2.1 Share Issue – Share Ca.	100,000	3.1 Purchase – Premises	50,000
		3.1 Purchase – Equipm.	10,000

Equipment Account

3.1 Purchase – Bank	10,000

Let's consider the next transaction:

3.1 Paid business rates for premises in cash for £500

 Ask: what's coming into the business, and what is going out – one tip – DO THE EASY PART FIRST!
Answer: cash is going out.

 Ask: where from?
Answer: the bank. So, we will make an entry in the Bank Account.

 Ask: which side? (note – allow time for answer).
Answer: the credit side. Thus:

Bank Account

2.1 Share Issue – Share Ca.	100,000	3.1 Purchase – Premises	50,000
		3.1 Purchase – Equipm.	10,000
		3.1 Cash – Business R.	500

 Ask: where is our debit entry going to go – what is coming into the business? *Answer:* the use of local services, for which we are paying business rates. So – let's open a Business Rates Account and debit the amount which we have spent.

Business Rates Account

3.1 Cash – Bank	500

We must also enter the name of the Business Rates Account in our first entry.

Bank Account

2.1 Share Issue – Share Ca.	100,000	3.1 Purchase – Premises	50,000
		3.1 Purchase – Equipm.	10,000
		3.1 Cash - Business R.	500

Pause and make sure everyone understands and agrees with what you have done so far.

Let's look at another transaction:

> 5.1 Purchase stock for £35,000 from M. Black on credit

☞ *Ask:* what is coming into the business and what is going out – get the easy part first!
Answer: stock is coming in. We will therefore open a Stock Account.
☞ *Ask:* where will our entry go?
Answer: on the debit (left-hand) side (because the stock is coming into the business). Draw a Stock Account on the flip-chart and make the debit entry (but do not name the credit entry account until after the next question).
☞ *Ask:* Okay – so what is going *out* of the business? (This may take a few seconds and one or two incorrect suggestions).
Answer: a liability to pay the supplier at a later date.
☞ *Ask:* what do we call someone we owe money to?
Answer: a creditor (people may well answer 'debtor' in error – make sure people understand the difference). So let's open a Creditors Account.
☞ *Ask:* where will our entry go?
Answer: on the credit (right-hand side). Yes, it must, because (a) it is a liability we have created, so is something of value which is going out of the business (even though the money won't physically go out until a later date, an IOU goes out, in effect, now) and (b) we have already made a debit entry in our Stock Account, so the other entry *must* be a credit one!

Stock Account

5.1 M. Black – Creditors	35,000

Creditors Account

5.1 M. Black – Stock	35,000

The next transaction is:

> 9.1 Sales of £15,000 to W. Smith for cash

☞ *Ask:* you know the form – what is coming in, what is going out, easiest part first?
Answer: money is coming in, so we debit the Bank Account.

Ask: what is going out?
Answer: sales – so we open a Sales Account and make a credit entry.

Note: people usually have problems with the credit entry, at first, until a full explanation is given. They think a sale is a good thing, therefore it must be coming into the business! They will also tend to want to credit the Stock Account. An explanation will be called for.

Money is coming into the business – as we agreed and entered in the Bank Account. Goods are going out, leaving the business, so although sales are a good thing the products are physically transferred into the customer's own-ership – and so have gone out of the business. However, we cannot credit our Stock Account.

 Ask: why not?
Answer: because stock was entered on the debit side when we purchased it and that was at cost price (cost to us). Sales are at selling price and so are nor-mally made up of cost plus a profit element. Because of our accounting convention of consistency, we must enter like with like within our accounts. We must therefore keep sales separate from stock. We will bring the two together at the end of a period when we calculate the profit earned, as we shall see later.

Someone may ask how we know what is in stock, because the stock account will now be inaccurate (having not taken account of the stock which left the business when the sale was made). The answer is that the only way we can be sure of what is left is by doing a stock-take.

Bank Account

2.1 Share Issue – Share Ca.	100,000	3.1 Purchase – Premises	50,000
9.1 W. Smith – Sales	15,000	3.1 Purchase – Equipm.	10,000
		3.1 Cash – Business R.	500

Sales Account

9.1 W. Smith - Bank	15,000

Notice that I have made the debit entry in the Bank Account on the first avail-able line, even though there is now an earlier entry on a lower line on the credit side of that account.

The next transaction is:

    10.1 Payment of wages £1,000

 Ask: same again – what's coming in, what's going out?
Answer: money is going out, so credit the Bank Account. The value of people's labour(whether you used it wisely or not) has been available to you and this was an expense to the business (as was the business rates transaction). We therefore open and debit a Salaries and Wages Account.

Bank Account

2.1 Share Issue – Share Ca.	100,000	3.1 Purchase – Premises	50,000
9.1 W. Smith – Sales	15,000	3.1 Purchase – Equipm.	10,000
		3.1 Cash – Business R.	500
		10.1 Wages – Salaries	1,000

Salaries and Wages Account

10.1 Wages – Bank	1,000

One thing you should always try and do; as soon as you have made the first entry, go on immediately to identify the second entry and make it properly. Otherwise, you can easily get distracted and the second entry will be missed.

Next transaction:

    10.1 Stock purchase for £45,000 from L. Drake on credit

 Ask: tell me what to do!
Answer: debit the Stock Account, credit the Creditors Account.

Stock Account

5.1 M. Black – Creditors	35,000
10.1 L. Drake – Creditors	45,000

Creditors Account

5.1 M. Black – Stock	35,000
10.1 L. Drake – Stock	45,000

Next transaction:

    12.1 Sales of £22,000 to E. Jones on credit

Ask: tell me what to do!

Answer: credit sales. Open a Debtors Account and make a debit entry. People may have initial problems with the latter. Draw their attention once again to the difference between Debtors and Creditors, as necessary. Also emphasise that a transaction 'on credit' in itself *does not* tell us whether credit or debit entries are made for the debt element, or whether goods are coming *into* or *out of* the business. This will depend on the nature of the transaction, i.e. is it a **sale** or a **purchase**?

Sales Account

9.1 W. Smith – Bank	15,000
12.1 E. Jones – Debtors	22,000

Debtors Account

12.1 E. Jones – Sales	22,000

Next transaction:

1.2 Payment of £35,000 to M. Black

 Ask: what do I do?

Answer: credit the Bank Account. Debit the Creditors Account. Debit the Creditors Account because we are reducing the total amount which the company owes by this sum (thus, in effect, a reduction of our debts to outside parties is coming into the business).

Bank Account

2.1 Share Issue – Share Ca.	100,000	3.1 Purchase – Premises	50,000
9.1 W. Smith – Sales	15,000	3.1 Purchase – Equipm.	10,000
		3.1 Cash – Business R.	500
		10.1 Wages – Salaries	1,000
		1.2 M. Black – Creditors	35,000

Creditors Account

1.2 M. Black – Bank	35,000	5.1 M. Black – Stock	35,000
		10.1 L. Drake – Stock	45,000

Next transaction:

☞ 2.2 Sales of £32,000 to K. Croft on credit

Ask: what do I do?
Answer: credit Sales, debit Debtors.

✎
Sales Account

9.1 W. Smith – Bank	15,000
12.1 E. Jones – Debtors	22,000
2.2 K. Croft – Debtors	32,000

Debtors Account

12.1 E. Jones – Sales	22,000
2.2 K. Croft – Sales	32,000

Next transaction:

5.2 Payment of £5,500 for printing and stationery

☞ *Ask:* what do I do?
Answer: credit Bank Account, open a Printing and Stationery Account and make a debit entry.

✎
Bank Account

2.1 Share Issue – Share Ca.	100,000	3.1 Purchase –Premises	50,000
9.1 W. Smith – Sales	15,000	3.1 Purchase – Equipm.	10,000
		3.1 Cash – Business R.	500
		10.1 Wages – Salaries	1,000
		1.2 M. Black – Creditors	35,000
		5.2 Purchase – Printing	5,500

Printing and Stationery Account

5.2 Purchase – Bank	5,500

Next transaction:

6.2 Payment for telephone calls £460

☞ *Ask:* well?
Answer: credit Bank Account, open a Telephone Account and make a debit entry.

Bank Account

2.1 Share Issue – Share Ca.	100,000	3.1 Purchase – Premises	50,000
9.1 W. Smith – Sales	15,000	3.1 Purchase – Equipm.	10,000
		3.1 Cash – Business R.	500
		10.1 Wages – Salaries	1,000
		1.2 M. Black – Creditors	35,000
		5.2 Purchase – Printing	5,500
		6.2 Calls – Telephone	460

Telephone Account

6.2 Calls – Bank	460

Let's have a look at one more transaction.

8.2 Payment received for £22,000 from E. Jones

 Ask: direct me!
Answer: debit Bank, credit Debtors.

Bank Account

2.1 Share Issue – Share Ca.	100,000	3.1 Purchase – Premises	50,000
9.1 W. Smith – Sales	15,000	3.1 Purchase – Equipm.	10,000
8.2 E. Jones – Debtors	22,000	3.1 Cash – Business R.	500
		10.1 Wages – Salaries	1,000
		1.2 M. Black – Creditors	35,000
		5.2 Purchase – Printing	5,500
		6.2 Calls – Telephone	460

Debtors Account

12.1 E. Jones – Sales	22,000	8.2 E. Jones – Bank	22,000
2.2 K. Croft – Sales	32,000		

We have now entered several transactions in the individual accounts. Let's go back and look at each account; I want you to tell me what *type* of account each one is.

Ask: what are the four types of account?
Answer: expenses, sales, assets and liabilities.
Ask: what is an asset?
Answer: something that has a value at the end of the period or at any given point in time (note that people may give specific examples, but it is important

to differentiate the nature of an asset).

☞ *Ask:* what is an expense?

Answer: something which has been used up during the course of the business period, i.e. it has no residual value.

☞ *Ask:* what is a liability?

Answer: something you owe to someone else, which involves paying them money at a later date.

Note: go through each account on the flip-chart, in the sequence in which they were written up, and ask the group which type of account each one is. Ensure that everyone fully understands the differences. This is a very important step, as it should really help to effectively consolidate their learning.

Account	Type
Bank	Asset
Share Capital	Liability (Long-Term!)
Premises	Asset
Equipment	Asset
Business Rates	Expense
Stock	Asset
Creditors	Liability
Sales	Sales (or Revenue)
Salaries and Wages	Expense
Debtors	Asset
Printing and Stationery	Expense
Telephone	Expense

☞ *Ask:* can you remember which two types of account will be transferred to the Trading, Profit and Loss Account at the end of the period – THINK carefully before you answer!

Answer: expenses and sales (don't give them the answer immediately if they get it wrong at first!).

☞ *Ask:* what types of account end up summarised in the Balance Sheet?

Answer: assets and liabilities.

Good. Now, I also mentioned earlier that the Trading, Profit and Loss Account is part of the double-entry system, while the Balance Sheet is not. We will look at how we transfer the expense and sales accounts to the Trading, Profit and Loss Account later – when we have looked specifically at the layout and purpose of that account. For now, we will just take another look at the asset and liability accounts. The balances on these accounts at the end of the period represent tangible current values. These accounts are kept **open**, ready for the start of the next period (unlike expense and sales accounts, which are **closed off** at the end of the period and the balances transferred to the Trading, Profit and Loss Account). Note that expenses and sales accounts totals do *not* represent current value; rather, they are a measure of what has been 'used up', i.e. gone out of or come into the business and is, therefore, no longer there. This point may help you further in understanding the crucial difference between expense and sales as opposed to asset and liability accounts.

I am now going to demonstrate how to balance off an asset account.

Let's look at the Bank Account first (turn to it on the flip-chart).

First, we decide which **side** of the account (debit or credit side) has the highest total. In this case, it is the debit side (otherwise we would have an overdraft situation, which would make this a liability, rather than an asset, account). We are going to leave a blank line below the last entry on the credit side, then total the left-hand side and write the entry in at the bottom.

Bank Account

2.1 Share Issue – Share Ca.	100,000	3.1 Purchase – Premises	50,000
9.1 W. Smith – Sales	15,000	3.1 Purchase – Equipm.	10,000
8.2 E. Jones – Debtors	22,000	3.1 Cash – Business R.	500
		10.1 Wages – Salaries	1,000
		1.2 M. Black – Creditors	35,000
		5.2 Purchase – Printing	5,500
		6.2 Calls – Telephone	460
	137,000		

We have now made a debit entry (£137,000), so we must make a corresponding credit entry. This time, however, it will be in the same account *and* on the same line, thus:

Bank Account

2.1 Share Issue – Share Ca.	100,000	3.1 Purchase – Premises	50,000
9.1 W. Smith – Sales	15,000	3.1 Purchase – Equipm.	10,000
8.2 E. Jones – Debtors	22,000	3.1 Cash – Business R.	500
		10.1 Wages – Salaries	1,000
		1.2 M. Black – Creditors	35,000
		5.2 Purchase – Printing	5,500
		6.2 Calls – Telephone	460
	137,000		137,000

So far, so good (people may take a while to understand and accept what you have done). However, we now have a problem; the debit side adds up to the £137,000, but the credit side does not – even though the credit total which we have just entered says that it should. What we need to do, therefore, is make a **closing balance** entry on the credit side, being the difference between the total (£137,000) and the total of the credit entries so far (which is £102,460). In other words, we need a balancing entry of £34,540.

Bank Account

2.1	Share Issue – Share Ca.	100,000	3.1 Purchase – Premises	50,000
9.1	W. Smith – Sales	15,000	3.1 Purchase – Equipm.	10,000
8.2	E. Jones – Debtors	22,000	3.1 Cash – Business R.	500
			10.1 Wages – Salaries	1,000
			1.2 M. Black – Creditors	35,000
			5.2 Purchase – Printing	5,500
			6.2 Calls – Telephone	460
			15.2 Closing Bal. c/f	34,540
		137,000		137,000

Both sides now add up to the total, but once more we have a problem; I have only made one entry, this time a credit one. What I must immediately do is make the corresponding debit entry. Once more, this will be in the same account, but this time underneath the balanced off total. It represents the opening balance at the start of the next period (16.2, since we have balanced the account off on 15.2). It is known as the **opening balance, brought forward** – you will notice that I termed the credit entry the **closing balance, carried forward** (explain the abbreviations).

Bank Account

2.1	Share Issue – Share Ca.	100,000	3.1 Purchase – Premises	50,000
9.1	W. Smith – Sales	15,000	3.1 Purchase – Equipm.	10,000
8.2	E. Jones – Debtors	22,000	3.1 Cash – Business R.	500
			10.1 Wages – Salaries	1,000
			1.2 M. Black – Creditors	35,000
			5.2 Purchase – Printing	5,500
			6.2 Calls – Telephone	460
			15.2 Closing Bal. c/f	34,540
		137,000		137,000
16.2	Opening Bal. b/f	34,540		

You can see that this account is an asset account because it has a debit balance. It has been balanced off at the end of the period (15.2), but remains open for the start of the following period (commencing 16.2). It should exactly equal the amount of money available to you in the bank at that date.

The next account is the Share Capital Account, which is a (long-term) liability account. We will balance that off, too.

Share Capital Account

15.2 Closing Bal. c/f	100,000	2.1 Share Issue – Bank	100,000
	100,000		100,000
		16.2 Opening Bal. b/f	100,000

Let's look at the next account, which is Premises. This is another asset account, but with just one entry, so it is easy to balance off.

Premises Account

3.1 Purchase – Bank	50,000	15.2 Closing Bal. c/f	50,000
	50,000		50,000
16.2 Opening Bal. b/f	50,000		

The next account, equipment, is dealt with in the same way.

Equipment Account

3.1 Purchase – Bank	10,000	15.2 Closing Bal. c/f	10,000
	10,000		10,000
16.2 Opening Bal. b/f	10,000		

The next account is Business Rates; this is an expense account, so we will leave it for the time being and move on to the next, which is Stock.

The Stock Account is slightly different, because it contains both an asset element (our current, or closing stock) and a type of expense. The expense aspect represents the stock which has gone out as sales, but at cost value, together with any stock which has been damaged or stolen. The asset element will be treated as before, i.e. balanced off and carried forward to the start of the next period. The expense aspect (known as **cost of sales**, or **cost of goods sold**), will be transferred (via the double-entry system) to the Trading, Profit and

Loss Account. Before we can do this, we must conduct a stock-take, in order to know what our closing stock is. The debit entries really represent opening stock (none, in this example) plus purchases.

This sum will equal the total amount of stock available for sale during the period. If we then credit the closing stock and balance off the account, the balancing figure will equal the **cost of sales**. This figure will be entered on the credit side, with the corresponding debit entry going into the Trading (first) section of the Trading, Profit and Loss Account, as follows:

Stock Account

5.1 M. Black – Creditors	35,000	
10.1 L. Drake – Creditors	45,000	

We conduct a stock-take and assess our closing stock as £21,000. We make the following entries:

Step One

Total the debit entries and make a corresponding total credit entry.

Stock Account

5.1 M. Black – Creditors	35,000		
10.1 L. Drake – Creditors	45,000		
	80,000		80,000

Step Two

Credit the closing stock and carry down the debit opening stock entry.

Stock Account

5.1 M. Black – Creditors	35,000	15.2 Closing Stock c/f	21,000
10.1 L. Drake – Creditors	45,000		
	80,000		80,000
16.2 Opening Stock b/f	21,000		

Step Three

Calculate the Cost of Sales and make the credit entry, then open the Trading, Profit and Loss Account and make the debit entry there.

Stock Account

5.1 M. Black – Creditors	35,000	15.2 Closing Stock c/f	21,000
10.1 L. Drake – Creditors	45,000	15.2 Cost of Sales – T.	59,000
	80,000		80,000
16.2 Opening Stock b/f	21,000		

Trading, Profit and Loss Account

15.2 Cost of Sales – Stock   59,000

We will deal with the Trading, Profit and Loss Account in the next session, but you will see that the logic of double-entry still works. The Stock Account has a debit balance and remains open (as an asset account).

Note: make sure everyone is happy with this procedure.

We will balance off one more account. The next in sequence is Creditors – a liability account:

Creditors Account

1.2 M. Black – Bank	35,000	5.1 M. Black – Stock	35,000
		10.1 L. Drake – Stock	45,000

We will balance it off as follows:

Creditors Account

1.2 M. Black – Bank	35,000	5.1 M. Black – Stock	35,000
15.2 Closing Bal. c/f	45,000	10.1 L. Drake – Stock	45,000
	80,000		80,000
		16.2 Opening Bal. b/f	45,000

Note that, being a liability account, Creditors has a closing *credit* balance.

I would like to summarise the key learning points which we have covered in this session:

- before you do anything else, make sure you *understand* what you are looking at and how it is drawn up

- there are four *types* of account

- expense and sales accounts represent a measure of value which has been used up during the period

- asset and liability accounts remain open at the end of the period because they *do* have a residual value

- expense and sales accounts are closed off and transferred to the Trading, Profit and Loss Account

- **assets** and **liabilities** are *listed* in the Balance Sheet but *not* transferred there

- a **creditor** is someone you owe money to

- a **debtor** owes you money and is therefore an asset

- a financial transaction involves an exchange of equal value between two entities

- the accounting entries made depend on which entity's eyes you are viewing the transaction through

- whatever comes *into* the business is debited to the appropriate account

- whatever is going *out of* the business is credited to the appropriate account

- your bank statement is viewed through the eyes of the bank; it is *their* statement, not yours

- keep 'sales' and 'stock' entries in separate accounts

There now follows an exercise which you can use to consolidate what you have learned and ensure that you really understand it (as opposed to merely believing that you do).

DOUBLE-ENTRY BOOKKEEPING

Exercise A – Question

From the following list of transactions, make the entries in the relevant accounts. When you have done this, balance off all the asset and liability accounts and transfer the cost of sales to the Trading, Profit and Loss Account.

6.4　Brian Lowe, sole trader, invests £80,000 in his new business

9.4　a bank loan for £30,000 is obtained

10.4　the business pays rent of £5,000

11.4　equipment is purchased for £6,000

11.4　printing and stationery is purchased for £3,000

13.4　stock is purchased on credit from M. Rose for £25,000

16.4　a credit sale of stock is made to G. Berry for £8,000

18.4　stock is purchased from A. Jest for £10,000 in cash

19.4　a credit sale to G. Farr is made for £15,000

23.4　wages are paid costing £4,000

23.4　a credit sale is made to T. Bent for £12,000

24.4　stock worth £20,000 is purchased on credit from D. Mann

25.4　£25,000 is paid to M. Rose

27.4　a credit sale is made to C. Lars for £16,000

30.4　payment of £5,000 is received from G. Berry

30.4　loan interest of £375 is paid

30.4　the equipment is depreciated by £125

30.4　a stock-take values goods at £17,500.

DOUBLE-ENTRY BOOKKEEPING

Exercise A – Answer

Bank Account

6.4	Investment – Capital	80,000	10.4	Cash – Rent	5,000
9.4	Cash – Bank Loan	30,000	11.4	Purchase – Equipm.	6,000
30.4	G. Berry – Debtors	5,000	11.4	Purchase – Printing	3,000
			18.4	A. Jest – Stock	10,000
			23.4	Cash – Wages	4,000
			25.4	M. Rose – Creditors	25,000
			30.4	Interest – Loan Int.	375
			30.4	Closing Bal. c/f	61,625
		115,000			115,000
1.5	Opening Bal. b/f	61,625			

Capital Account

30.4	Closing Bal. c/f	80,000	6.4	Investment – Bank	80,000
		80,000			80,000
			1.5	Opening Bal. b/f	80,000

Bank Loan Account

30.4	Closing Bal. c/f	30,000	9.4	Cash – Bank	30,000
		30,000			30,000
			1.5	Opening Bal. b/f	30,000

Rent Account

10.4	Cash – Bank	5,000

Equipment Account

11.4	Purchase – Bank	6,000	30.4	Write-off – Deprec.	125
			30.4	Closing Bal. c/f	5,875
		6,000			6,000
1.5	Opening Bal. b/f	5,875			

Printing and Stationery Account

11.4 Purchase – Bank	3,000	

Stock Account

13.4 M. Rose – Creditors	25,000	30.4 Closing Stock c/f	17,500
18.4 A. Jest – Bank	10,000	30.4 Cost of Sales – T.	37,500
24.4 D. Mann – Creditors	20,000		
	55,000		55,000
1.5 Opening Stock b/f	17,500		

Creditors Account

25.4 M. Rose – Bank	25,000	13.4 M. Rose – Stock	25,000
30.4 Closing Bal. c/f	20,000	24.4 D. Mann – Stock	20,000
	45,000		45,000
		1.5 Opening Bal. b/f	20,000

Sales Account

	16.4 G. Berry – Debtors	8,000
	19.4 G. Farr – Debtors	15,000
	23.4 T. Bent – Debtors	12,000
	27.4 C. Lars – Debtors	16,000

Debtors Account

16.4 G. Berry – Sales	8,000	30.4 G. Berry – Bank	5,000
19.4 G. Farr – Sales	15,000	30.4 Closing Bal. c/f	46,000
23.4 T. Bent – Sales	12,000		
27.4 C. Lars – Sales	16,000		
	51,000		51,000
1.5 Opening Bal. b/f	46,000		

Wages Account

23.4 Cash – Bank	4,000	

Loan Interest Account

30.4 Interest – Bank	375	

Depreciation Account

30.4 Write-off – Equipment   125

Trading, Profit and Loss Account

30.4 Cost of Sales – Stock   37,500

Notes

G. Berry (a debtor) still owes us £3,000. This is easily checked when a correct double-entry system is used.

Session 3

···

Have we done well?

In the last session, we looked at how each financial transaction is recorded in the accounts via the double-entry system. This will provide us with the essential foundation for assessing the performance and health of the organisation at any point thereafter. Most people have heard of (and probably seen) a Trading, Profit and Loss Account.

👉 *Ask:* what do you think is the purpose of this account?
Answer: in essence, to see if we are making a profit and, if so, how much.

👉 *Ask:* how do you think this can be achieved?
Answer: (may need some prompting) by seeing what's left over after taking all our costs away from our income.

👉 *Ask:* where does the information which we need to work this out come from?
Answer: the sales and expense accounts.

👉 *Ask:* as opposed to which other types of accounts?
Answer: the asset and liability accounts.

In effect, the Trading, Profit and Loss Account is a giant calculator. We programme in all the sales on one side of the account, then enter the various expenses on the other. The difference is the balance between the two sides of the account and represents the overall profit or loss for the period covered by the sales and expenses which have been summarised there.

We mentioned during the last session that the Trading, Profit and Loss Account (unlike the Balance Sheet) is part of the double-entry system. We also saw how we would transfer the cost of sales into it when balancing off the Stock Account. Since we are probably hoping to make a profit, it is logical to start with the biggest entry – sales. We therefore need to close off the Sales Account (in our example there was just one) and transfer the balance to the Trading, Profit and Loss Account.

👉 *Ask:* which side of the Trading, Profit and Loss Account will the sales balance end up on?
Answer: the credit side. There was a credit balance on the Sales Account, so we

would make a corresponding debit entry in that account to close it off; the Trading, Profit and Loss Account would therefore have to receive a credit entry for sales as the second part of that double-entry transfer.

Note: turn back to the flip-chart entries for the example in the previous session.

Sales Account

9.1 W. Smith – Bank	15,000
12.1 E. Jones – Debtors	22,000
2.2 K. Croft - Debtors	32,000

This was the Sales Account when we left it. First, we total the largest side (in this case, the credit side) and make entries on each side of the account.

Sales Account

	9.1 W. Smith – Bank	15,000
	12.1 E. Jones – Debtors	22,000
	2.2 K. Croft – Debtors	32,000
69,000		69,000

Next, we make the debit entry to balance the debit total; the corresponding entry will transfer this balance to the credit side of the Trading, Profit and Loss Account.

Sales Account

15.2 Closing Bal. – Trading,	69,000	9.1 W. Smith – Bank	15,000
		12.1 E. Jones – Debtors	22,000
		2.2 K. Croft – Debtors	32,000
	69,000		69,000

Trading, Profit and Loss Account

15.2 Cost of Sales	59,000	15.2 Closing Bal. – Sa.	69,000

Point out that we had already transferred the cost of sales into the Trading, Profit and Loss Account from the Stock Account. It can now been seen that sales and costs are going to end up on opposite sides of the Trading, Profit and Loss Account.

Ask: now, what is the difference between the Sales Account and the Stock Account?

Answer: the first is a sales (or revenue) account, the second is an asset account. In fact, the Sales Account is now closed. It is, in effect, empty – it has no out-standing balance. When we look at our Stock Account, however, it remains open, with an opening debit balance at the start of the next period.

Stock Account

5.1 M. Black – Creditors	35,000	15.2 Closing Stock c/f	21,000
10.1 L. Drake – Creditors	45,000	15.2 Cost of Sales – T.	59,000
	80,000		80,000
16.2 Opening Stock b/f	21,000		

Let's reconsider the Trading, Profit and Loss Account. What we are actually doing is summarising the total sales (or revenue) accounts on the credit side, while summarising the totals of all the various expense accounts on the debit side. However, a certain format is necessary and you need to understand it. So far, we have made just two entries.

Ask: what are you left with if you take the cost of sales away from sales?
Answer: (they may have trouble at first) profit.

Ask: what *kind* of profit?
Answer: GROSS profit. Cost of sales is quite a different type of cost or expense to all the others, for various reasons. It is very important to understand this.

Sales – Cost of Sales = Gross Profit

In effect, we have taken what we received in terms of money for the goods which we sold and subtracted the cost of those goods to us, i.e. what we paid for them. Remember, gross profit is what we got for the goods, less what they cost us (including any that were lost, stolen or destroyed in the process). Gross profit is therefore the profit element which is purely attributable to the *trading* which we have done. It takes no account of any overhead costs which may also need to be deducted.

Note: pause to ensure that this point sinks in.

Now, perhaps you can see why the proper title of a profit and loss account is the Trading, Profit and Loss Account. What we will now do is balance off our account at this stage to calculate the gross profit.

Trading, Profit and Loss Account

15.2 Cost of Sales	59,000	15.2 Closing Bal. – Sa.	69,000
15.2 Gross Profit c/d	10,000		
	69,000		69,000
		15.2 Gross Profit b/d	10,000

The abbreviation for 'carried down' is c/d, b/d for 'brought down'. What we have done is to balance off the trading section of the account. We are left with a credit balance, which represents gross profit.

 Ask: what do we need to take off from gross profit to arrive at *net* profit? *Answer:* all the other expenses. In fact, the other expenses in our example are all **operating** expenses. That means they are all expenses which arose as normal costs of operating the business. So, we need to balance off each expense account and transfer the figures into the next section of our Trading, Profit and Loss Account.

Business Rates Account

3.1 Cash – Bank	500	15.2 Closing Bal. – Tra.	500
	500		500

Salaries and Wages Account

10.1 Wages – Bank	1,000	15.2 Closing Bal. – Tra.	1,000
	1,000		1,000

Printing and Stationery Account

5.2 Purchase – Bank	5,500	15.2 Closing Bal. – Tra.	5,500
	5,500		5,500

Telephone Account

6.2 Calls – Bank	460	15.2 Closing Bal. – Tra.	460
	460		460

Trading, Profit and Loss Account

15.2 Cost of Sales – Stock	59,000	15.2 Closing Bal. – Sales	69,000
15.2 Gross Profit c/d	10,000		
	69,000		69,000
15.2 Business Rates – Bal.	500	15.2 Gross Profit b/d	10,000
15.2 Salaries and Wages – Ba.	1,000		
15.2 Printing and Stationery	5,500		
15.2 Telephone – Bal.	460		

 Ask: are there any other expenses in our example?

Answer: no; all the other accounts are asset or liability accounts. We can now, therefore, calculate our net profit (or net loss!).

Trading, Profit and Loss Account

15.2 Cost of Sales – Stock	59,000	15.2 Closing Bal. – Sales	69,000
15.2 Gross Profit c/d	10,000		
	69,000		69,000
15.2 Business Rates – Bal.	500	15.2 Gross Profit b/d	10,000
15.2 Salaries and Wages – Ba.	1,000		
15.2 Printing and Stationery	5,500		
15.2 Telephone – Bal.	460		
15.2 Net Profit c/d	2,540		
	10,000		10,000
		15.2 Net profit b/d	2,540

The remaining credit balance represents net profit – what is left over from sales after **all** expenses have been deducted. Since the business is not concerned with making a profit for itself, the profit actually belongs to the owners; until it is paid to them, it is a **liability** to the business. That part still retained after drawings or dividends are paid to the owner(s) is a long-term liability.

Note: the concept that net profit is a liability may throw people briefly, as they usually think of it as a *good* thing. You could point out if this occurs that it is similar to their initial concept that debtors are a bad thing, yet they now know why debtors are an **asset**!

☞ *Ask:* what is a Trading, Profit and Loss Account?
Answer: a calculator to work out overall profit or loss.
☞ *Ask:* what is **gross profit**?
Answer: sales minus cost of sales.
☞ *Ask:* what are **operating expenses**?
Answer: expenses (excluding cost of sales) normally incurred in running the business.
☞ *Ask:* what is **net profit**?
Answer: gross profit minus operating expenses (also after any extraordinary expenses, or costs incurred by the business but not in respect of its normal operation), or, sales minus ALL costs.

We have been looking at the Trading, Profit and Loss Account as it originally evolved. This was with the same debit and credit sides as all the other accounts. Our example is therefore set out in what is termed a **horizontal** format, which makes it easier to see how entries are transferred into it on each side using normal double-entry procedures. However, the Trading, Profit and Loss Account is normally presented in a different way. This is known as the **vertical** format, and follows the following sequence (go through the list and explain each heading).

Sales	$\left(\begin{array}{l} \text{This is the} \\ \text{Trading section} \end{array} \right)$
− Cost of Sales	
= Gross Profit	
− All Operating Costs	
= Operating Profit	
+ Any Other Revenue	
=	
− Any Other Costs	
= Net Profit Before Tax	
− Income or Corporation Tax	
= Net Profit After Tax	

Any Other Revenue would be income not really generated from the normal trading activity or purpose of the business, e.g. income from letting a spare room for an organisation whose primary purpose is to make a profit from manufacturing. Any Other Costs would have arisen from something similarly unconnected to the main trading purpose of the organisation, e.g. agency costs for rent collection in respect of the spare room letting. In many cases there will be no other revenue or costs and Operating Profit will be the same as Net Profit Before Tax. This is the case in our working example, which we can now present in a vertical format:-

Trading, Profit and Loss Account for the Period 1.1 – 15.2

	%	£	£
Sales			69,000
Cost of Sales	85.51		59,000
Gross Profit	14.49		10,000
Operating Expenses			
Business Rates	0.72	500	
Salaries and Wages	1.45	1,000	
Printing and Stationery	7.97	5,500	
Telephone	0.67	460	
			7,460
Net Profit			2,540

☞ *Ask:* what did we say the *first* thing is that you should do when presented with a table of figures?

Answer: make sure we know where they come from and how they are worked out. We now understand where all the account names and terminology comes from (make sure everyone does). First of all, notice that the Trading, Profit and Loss Account summarises all the sales and expense accounts *for a given period*. This is quite different from the Balance Sheet and is very useful to remember and understand.

Following on from each item, the first column is a percentage column.

☞ *Ask:* what does each percentage figure represent?
Answer: the percentage which that item represents to Sales.

☞ *Ask:* work out the percentage that Net Profit is to Sales.
Answer: 3.68 per cent.

Note: make absolutely sure that *everyone* has worked this out properly (*before* you agree the answer!). The ability to work with percentage calculations is crucial so it is very important to be certain that everyone can do this using their own particular calculators. In fact, it is possible to calculate the figure by adding the other percentage figures (other than Gross Profit) and subtracting from 100, *or* by adding the Operating Expenses percentages and subtracting the sum from the Gross Profit percentage. It would be useful to demonstrate these methods afterwards. However, the method we are checking here is as follows:

Net Profit divided by Sales × 100

$$= \frac{2,540}{69,000} \times 100$$

 Ask: why bother working out the percentage column?
Answer: so we can compare relative individual expenses and/or how expenses have changed from a previous period and/or budget.

The second column is not a debit column; it is a sub-total column only (explain this carefully, for it is usually an initial source of confusion to trainees).

The final column is the grand totals column, where total sales and costs are combined to calculate Net Profit or Loss.

The vertical format is the one seen in an organisation's annual report. It is a clearer way of following the calculations through to arrive at the net surplus or deficit. This will be the same for any organisation, whether profit-oriented or not. Social clubs, charities, public sector organisations and so on will all use a similar presentation, although the title may be different, e.g. Income And Expenditure Account.

Where there are many expense accounts, they are often categorised under appropriate sub-headings below 'Operating Expenses', e.g. Administration, Sales (expenses such as Advertising and Display would come under this sub-heading), Finance and so on.

There is one situation that we haven't considered. This is where the organisation does not simply buy in stock and re-sell it, but manufactures its own products for sale. In this situation, there will be an additional account in the double-entry accounts. This is called, appropriately enough, the Manufacturing Account! It operates very like the Trading, Profit and Loss Account, in that it brings together all the individual cost accounts which are involved in the **manufacturing** side of the business, calculates the totals and arrives at the cost of finished goods which were produced and made available for sale (whether actually sold in the period or not).

Let's suppose that, instead of purchasing stock in our example, the company manufactured it. Its Manufacturing Account would look something like this:

Manufacturing Account

	£	£
Raw Materials 1.1		1,100
Purchases		14,200
		15,300
Less Raw Materials at 15.2		1,200
Cost of Raw Material Consumed		14,100
Direct Wages		34,300
Direct Expenses		2,600
Prime Cost		51,000
Factory Overhead Expenses		
Rent	3,000	
Rates	500	
Fuel and Power	1,250	
Indirect Wages	19,500	
Depreciation of Plant	500	
Insurance	750	
Lubricants	200	
General Factory Expenses	1,500	
		27,200
		78,200
Work in Progress 1.1		5,300
		83,500
Less, Work in Progress at 15.2		3,500
Production Cost of Goods Completed		80,000

Here again, we have a sub-total column, but this time we are trying to calculate the total cost to us of **producing** the completed goods which we manufactured, ready for sale. We therefore *add* the expenses rather than subtracting them because we are *not* trying to calculate a profit element. We have calculated stock of raw materials in the same way, in effect, as we did in our original stock account:

	Opening Stock
Plus	Purchases
Minus	Closing Stock

Direct wages are paid to people whose labour is specifically attributable to the production of particular units, e.g. a machine operator. **Indirect wages** are paid to people whose work cannot be allocated to a particular item which is being produced, e.g. a security guard. **Direct expenses** could be things like royalties which must be paid for each item as it is manufactured.

We have assumed that work in progress at the start is completed during the period, so we have added it to our total production cost of goods completed. We have deducted uncompleted goods, i.e. work in progress at the close of the period.

Stocks of raw materials and work in progress at the end of the period are **assets** and so a manufacturing company would include them in its Balance Sheet. However, our example is not a manufacturing company (since none of our example transactions related to a manufacturing account as shown above). If there had been a manufacturing process, then the figures appearing in the Manufacturing Account would have been derived from the appropriate individual accounts resulting from the relevant transactions. This example of the Manufacturing Account is merely to demonstrate how it works and show that similar double-entry rules would apply.

The final figure in the Manufacturing Account (£80,000) is the same as the amount that we have purchased in our working example. This example would therefore be the same once the entries were made for the cost of completed goods manufactured in place of the goods purchased for resale. For simplicity, we will revert back to our original example in future and assume that the company has *purchased* stock as opposed to *manufacturing* it.
Note: although this may look complicated, trainees do not usually have any problems with this explanation. It is useful to give it where people are working in a manufacturing environment.

I would like to summarise the key learning points we have covered in this session:

- the Trading, Profit and Loss Account **summarises** sales and expense accounts and **calculates** overall Net Profit or Loss

- it **is** an integral part of the double-entry system

- **Gross** Profit equals Sales minus Cost of Sales

- Gross Profit **minus** Operating Expenses equals **Operating** Profit

- Operating Profit plus any other revenue, minus any other costs, leaves **Net Profit** (or Loss!)

- any Net Profit is owed by the company to the owners

- undistributed Net Profit is, therefore, a long term **liability** to the company

- the Trading, Profit and Loss Account is displayed in a **vertical** format

- always make sure you fully understand how it is drawn up and what the figures represent before trying to use them

- the format of the account is similar whatever type of organisation is involved, but it may have a different title

- manufacturing companies will need a Manufacturing Account to calculate the cost of completed goods produced during the period

- the Manufacturing Account is **also** part of the double-entry system

- manufacturing companies will have stocks of raw materials *and* work in progress in addition to stocks of completed goods. All of these are **Assets**

TRADING, PROFIT AND LOSS ACCOUNT

Exercise B – Question

Go back to the answer to Exercise A. Using the double-entry system, draw up the Trading, Profit and Loss Account for the period using the **horizontal** format. Once completed, draw it up in a **vertical** format, incorporating a percentage column.

TRADING, PROFIT AND LOSS ACCOUNT

Exercise B – Answer

Horizontal Format

Sales Account

30.4	Closing Bal. – Trading,	51,000	16.4	G. Berry – Debtors	8,000
			19.4	G. Farr – Debtors	15,000
			23.4	T. Bent – Debtors	12,000
			27.4	C. Lars – Debtors	16,000
		51,000			51,000

Trading, Profit and Loss Account

30.4	Cost of Sales – Stock	37,500	30.4	Closing Bal. – Sa.	51,000
30.4	Gross Profit c/d	13,500			
		51,000			51,000
30.4	Rent – Bal.	5,000	30.4	Gross Profit b/d	13,500
30.4	Printing and Stationery	3,000			
30.4	Wages – Bal.	4,000			
30.4	Loan Interest – Bal.	375			
30.4	Depreciation – Bal.	125			
30.4	Net Profit c/d	1,000			
		13,500			13,500
			30.4	Net Profit b/d	1,000

Rent Account

10.4	Cash – Bank	5,000	30.4	Closing Bal. – Tra.	5,000
		5,000			5,000

Printing and Stationery Account

11.4	Purchase – Bank	3,000	30.4	Closing Bal. – Tra.	3,000
		3,000			3,000

Wages Account

23.4 Cash – Bank	4,000	30.4 Closing Bal. – Tra.	4,000
	4,000		4,000

Loan Interest Account

30.4 Interest – Bank	375	30.4 Closing Bal. – Tradi.	375
	375		375

Depreciation Account

30.4 Write-off – Equipment	125	30.4 Closing Bal. – Tradi.	125
	125		125

Vertical Format

Trading, Profit and Loss Account for the Period 6.4 – 30.4

	%	£	£
Sales			51,000
Cost of Sales	73.53		37,500
Gross Profit	26.47		13,500
Operating Expenses			
Rent	9.80	5,000	
Printing and Stationery	5.88	3,000	
Wages	7.84	4,000	
Loan Interest	0.74	375	
Depreciation	0.25	125	
			12,500
Net Profit	1.96		1,000

Notes

As explained in Exercise A, Depreciation and Loan Interest are expense accounts. In this case, depreciation is the *only* expense which does not involve an actual outflow of funds; it is a book transfer, reflecting the devaluation of the asset from which it was derived.

Session 4

· ·

Where are we now?

The Trading, Profit and Loss Account tells us whether we end up with a surplus or deficit of income over expenditure for the period it covers. There are very important things, however, that it does *not* tell us. For instance, how much **cash** is available to us *now*, how much we have in stock and many other important pieces of information. To find these things, we need to look elsewhere; that is where the **Balance Sheet** comes in.

Ask: what are we going to find if we look at a Balance Sheet?
Answer: all the assets and liabilities. There are two very important differences between the Balance Sheet and the Trading, Profit and Loss Account which will help you enormously if you can understand them now and remember them in the future: ·

Balance Sheet	Trading, Profit and Loss Account
1 is *not* part of the double-entry system	*is* part of the double-entry system
2 shows us the situation *at a given point in time*	shows what has happened *over a certain period of time*

The significance of the second point will become clearer shortly. Let's start by drawing up the Balance Sheet for the example transactions we used earlier. Before we do, I will explain one or two things about the layout.

Just like the Trading, Profit and Loss Account, the original layout of the Balance Sheet was in a **horizontal** layout. And, just like the Trading, Profit and Loss Account, the Balance Sheet is now laid out **vertically**. We will begin, as we did with the Trading, Profit and Loss Account, by drawing up the traditional, horizontal layout. Doing it this way first is very useful, because it shows us how the Balance Sheet works.

We must go back to all the asset and liability accounts (turn back to the original example on the flip-chart). These remained **open**, because there was a

residual value for these items. The residual values are **closing balances**. It is these closing balances (which are also the **opening balances** for the start of the next period) which are listed in the Balance Sheet. Note that I have said *listed*, and not *transferred*; remember, the Balance Sheet is *not* part of the double-entry system. We simply **copy** the closing balances into the Balance Sheet.

As with the Trading, Profit and Loss Account, the Balance Sheet follows a certain **format**. The first rule to remember is that the assets and liabilities, while appearing on opposite *sides* in the **horizontal** format, are listed in reverse order of liquidity. This simply means that the *least* liquid are entered *first*. **Liquid** means the degree to which an item is in cash form (cash being the most liquid). Whatever takes the longest to turn into cash is the least liquid item. Using our example, we shall start by listing the assets.

 Ask: which is the *least* liquid asset in our example?
Answer: Premises. So, let's start by entering this in our Balance Sheet:

Balance Sheet as at 15.2

Fixed Assets
Premises   50,000

Now for something totally illogical. You will notice that the entry is made on the **credit** side, even though we have always placed asset balances on the debit side in our accounts. For some reason, whoever dreamed up the original layout for a Balance Sheet thought they would confuse everyone by *reversing* the debit and credit entries! This would not be possible if the Balance Sheet *was* part of the double-entry system; since it is *not*, we can put things wherever we like.

You will notice that I have put a heading, '**Fixed Assets**'. An asset is fixed if it is likely to last longer than a given trading period. Often, as with premises, it will remain in existence in its current form for many years – although not necessarily at the same value.

 Ask: what is the next *least* liquid asset?
Answer: equipment.
 Ask: is equipment a *fixed* asset?
Answer: yes. So, let's list that next, underneath premises.

Balance Sheet as at 15.2

Fixed Assets
Premises   50,000
Equipment   10,000

59

Ask: what is the next *least* liquid asset?

Answer: stock.

 Ask: is stock a *fixed* asset?

Answer: no; it will usually be used up and replaced several times during a full trading period (usually a year). With an asset like this, we use a different description. I am going to subtotal the fixed assets and put stock (and the other remaining assets) under a new heading.

Balance Sheet as at 15.2

Fixed Assets		
Premises	50,000	
Equipment	10,000	
		60,000
Current Assets		
Stock	21,000	

 Ask: what is the next *least* liquid **current** asset?

Answer: debtors. Remember, they are an asset, not a liability. Like stock, they will normally be **realised** (turned into cash) and replaced several times in a full period.

Balance Sheet as at 15.2

Fixed Assets		
Premises	50,000	
Equipment	10,000	
		60,000
Current Assets		
Stock	21,000	
Debtors	32,000	

 Ask: are there any other assets?

Answer: yes – bank. Let's put that in next.

Balance Sheet as at 15.2

Fixed Assets		
Premises	50,000	
Equipment	10,000	
		60,000
Currents Assets		
Stock	21,000	
Debtors	32,000	
Bank	34,540	
		87,540

☞ *Ask:* are there any other assets?
Answer: no! In our accounts, bank is the most liquid asset of all. In fact, the only other asset which is likely to be more liquid in any organisation is *cash in hand*!

Let's turn our attention now to the liabilities, which we will list on the other side of the Balance Sheet.

☞ *Ask:* what is the *least* liquid liability? (This may prove a little more difficult at first.)
Answer: it is, in fact, *share capital*. This is because, of all liabilities, capital will be paid out last. It is also a liability because, as we said previously, the organisation is a separate entity to the owner(s) and therefore owes them the money which they originally invested in the business. It is given its own heading (capital) because of its particular (long-term) nature.

Balance Sheet as at 15.2

Capital		Fixed Assets		
Share Capital	100,000	Premises	50,000	
		Equipment	10,000	
				60,000
		Current Assets		
		Stock	21,000	
		Debtors	32,000	
		Bank	34,540	
				87,540

Now, there is another very important thing to consider at this stage. In our Trading, Profit and Loss Account, we calculated that the company had made a net profit of £2,540.

☞ *Ask:* who does this belong to?
Answer: the owners. Remember, the organisation is not concerned with ending up *in itself* better or worse off than when it started. If it ends up with a surplus, this surplus has to eventually be paid to the people who invested in the organisation in the first place. Similarly, a deficit would have to be charged to the owners.

Now, I have repeatedly emphasised that the Trading, Profit and Loss Account *is* part of the double-entry system. In fact, it is *not* closed off; it has an outstanding balance of the £2,540 net profit, which has *not* been paid to the owners. This figure is a **credit** balance in the account, and – as we have seen – is a liability to the business. We therefore have to list it in the Balance Sheet. We place it as the next item, since it belongs to the owners.

Balance Sheet as at 15.2

Capital			*Fixed Assets*		
Share Capital	100,000		Premises	50,000	
Net Profit	2,540		Equipment	10,000	
		102,540			60,000
			Current Assets		
			Stock	21,000	
			Debtors	32,000	
			Bank	34,540	
					87,540

Note: pause and make sure everyone is clear about this very important point.

If this business was a sole trader, we could add share capital and undistributed Net Profit and show them as one figure. However, this business is a limited company. We know that because it started by issuing shares. Limited companies *must* show the original capital which was subscribed through the issue of shares separately from undistributed profit and any other items which may also belong to the owners.

 Ask: what is the next liability which we must list in the Balance Sheet? *Answer:* creditors. In fact, this is the *only* individual account left to deal with. Creditors, like debtors, are normally 'used up' and replaced several times per year. They are, therefore, also **current** and will be listed under a sub-heading in a similar way.

Balance Sheet as at 15.2

Capital			*Fixed Assets*		
Share Capital	100,000		Premises	50,000	
Net Profit	2,540		Equipment	10,000	
		102,540			60,000
Current Liabilities			*Current Assets*		
Creditors		45,000	Stock	21,000	
			Debtors	32,000	
			Bank	34,540	
					87,540

We have now listed *all* the assets and liabilities as at 15.2. The only thing which remains is to add both sides and make sure it **balances!**

Balance Sheet as at 15.2

Capital			*Fixed Assets*		
Share Capital	100,000		Premises	50,000	
Net Profit	2,540		Equipment	10,000	
		102,540			60,000
Current Liabilities			*Current Assets*		
Creditors		45,000	Stock	21,000	
			Debtors	32,000	
			Bank	34,540	
					87,540
		147,540			147,540

Phew! It does! That's always a nice feeling!

Now that we have drawn up our traditional-style Balance Sheet, let's just see how it works. First, as we can see, it balances. It shows us what the **total assets** are – £147,540. It shows us how much of these are **fixed** and how much are **current**. It tells us how the organisation's assets are being funded. In this case, they are being funded (or financed) by the owners (£102,540) and the creditors (£45,000). It also shows us *how* the owners' 'share' is made up.

Let's consider this last point further and see how changes affect our Balance Sheet. Let us suppose that the premises were **revalued**. In the individual accounts, the Premises Account would be debited by the amount of the increase; the corresponding credit entry would be made to a Revaluation Reserve Account.

Premises Account

3.1 Purchase – Bank	50,000	15.2 Closing Bal. c/f	60,000
15.2 Revaluation	10,000		
	60,000		60,000
16.2 Opening Bal. b/f	60,000		

Revaluation Reserve Account

16.2 Closing Bal. c/f	10,000	15.2 Revaluation – Pre.	10,000
	10,000		10,000
		16.2 Opening Bal. b/f	10,000

In our Balance Sheet, a fixed asset – premises – would be increased to reflect its new value (and the new closing balance value in the Premises Account). Note that **revaluation** is shown as a separate **increase** to the original value; **depreciation** would have been shown as a separate **deduction**.

If we have increased an asset, there must be either a corresponding decrease in another asset (e.g. bank) or a similar increase in a liability – according to how the increase in the asset has been financed. In this case, no money has changed hands; the increase in value has come about purely because of inflation. As we have seen in the case of Net Profit, the *business* is not concerned with accumulating a surplus – any such surplus belongs to the *owners*.This surplus is, therefore, an additional liability of the organisation under the **capital** section of the Balance Sheet.

Balance Sheet as at 15.2

Capital			Fixed Assets		
Share Capital	100,000		Premis. 50,000		
Revaluation Reserve	10,000		Revalu. 10,000		
Net Profit	2,540			60,000	
		112,540	Equipment	10,000	
Current Liabilities					70,000
Creditors		45,000	Current Assets		
			Stock	21,000	
			Debtors	32,000	
			Bank	34,540	
					87,540
		157,540			157,540

There are a couple of things to note about these entries. First, the revaluation is a **reserve**. Although it is a surplus which is ultimately owed to the owners, it will only become real when the asset from which it derived is sold. In the meantime, we cannot even be certain that it exists; the only time we really know what something is worth is when we actually sell it. Therefore, because the reserve is not an actual amount of spendable money – and because of our accounting convention of **conservatism** – this reserve will *not* be distributed to the shareholders (at least until the asset is sold).

Net profit may also be termed a **reserve**, but this *may* be distributed to the owners at a later time. When drawing up the Balance Sheet, it is possible to have a sub-heading for reserves. Remember, though, that all reserves belong to the owners of the business (unless all the assets are insufficient to repay the other liabilities when an organisation is wound up, in which case the owners will have the last claim on whatever is left over; this might happen where the asset values in the Balance Sheet exceed their real values).

Let's see what would happen to the Balance Sheet if we pay a dividend.

☞ *Ask:* how would our last Balance Sheet be affected?

Answer: bank would go down; net profit retained in the business would also decrease. Let's suppose that we pay dividends of £500:

Balance Sheet as at 15.2

Capital			*Fixed Assets*			
Share Capital	100,000		Premis. 50,000			
Revaluation Reserve	10,000		Revalu. 10,000			
Net Profit 2,540					60,000	
Dividend 500			Equipment		10,000	
	2,040					70,000
		112,040	*Current Assets*			
Current Liabilities			Stock		21,000	
Creditors		45,000	Debtors		32,000	
			Bank		34,040	
						87,040
		157,040				157,040

Let's carry on from here, and consider how another transaction would affect our new Balance Sheet. Let's suppose that we make a sale on credit for £10,000 and that the sale has a Gross Profit element of 20 per cent.

☞ *Ask:* what is going to change on our Balance Sheet?

Answer: stock will decrease by sales – gross profit (which equals the cost of goods sold). In this case, therefore, stock will decrease by £8,000. Off setting this decrease in one asset (stock), however, will be an increase in another; debtors will increase by the full sales value of £10,000. If we only make these two changes, the Balance Sheet will no longer balance, because we have increased debtors by £2,000 more than we have decreased stock. This is because stock is valued on a different basis to sales. The difference is the gross profit. Since there have been no additional operating expenses, the gross profit in *this* case will also be the net profit.

☞ *Ask:* who does the net profit belong to?

Answer: the owners. It is therefore a **liability** (as we know) and in this case, therefore, net profit will be increased by £2,000 – thereby offsetting the over-all £2,000 increase in asset values on the other side of the Balance Sheet.

Balance Sheet as at 15.2

Capital			*Fixed Assets*		
Share Capital	100,000		Premis. 50,000		
Revaluation Reserve	10,000		Revalu. 10,000		
Net Profit 4,540				60,000	
Dividend 500			Equipment	10,000	
	4,040				70,000
		114,040	*Current Assets*		
Current Liabilities			Stock	13,000	
Creditors		45,000	Debtors	42,000	
			Bank	34,040	
					89,040
		159,040			159,040

The Balance Sheet still balances. In fact, whatever transactions occur, it will *always* balance! The total assets (final total) figure will change, but it will still balance. This is because:

Assets = Capital + Liabilities

This simple relationship creates a formula, which means that we can always calculate a missing figure provided we have the other two. Whichever way round we use this formula, it always applies:

Assets – Liabilities = Capital
or
Assets – Capital = Liabilities

We can now clearly see why the Balance Sheet shows the position of an organisation only at a specific point in time. Whenever a transaction takes place, the assets and liabilities will change and this will automatically alter the balance sheet accordingly.

Note: make sure that everyone is clear and happy with what you have gone through with them on Balance Sheets before moving on.

We shall now look at the layout of the Balance Sheet in a **vertical** format. We will go back to our original example and draw up the Balance Sheet thus:

Balance Sheet as at 15.2

	£	£
Fixed Assets		
Premises	50,000	
Equipment	10,000	
		60,000
Current Assets		
Stock	21,000	
Debtors	32,000	
Bank	34,540	
	87,540	
Current Liabilities		
Creditors	45,000	
Working Capital		42,540
Net Assets		102,540
Financed by:		
Share Capital	100,000	
Undistributed Net Profit	2,540	
		102,540
		102,540

Once again, with the **vertical** format the columns are for subtotal and total figures; they are *not* debit and credit SIDES.

 Ask: can you see an advantage in this layout?

Answer: it is easier to follow; you don't have to look across from one side to the other. It also throws up some very important figures which were *not* immediately obvious from the equivalent **horizontal** format. Two terms are of particular importance and you should become very familiar with them if the Balance Sheet is to be of great use to you. The first is

Working Capital,

which is Current Assets *minus* Current Liabilities.

This of great importance, because it tells us how much surplus *liquid* funds we have in the organisation. If we don't have enough, we could be in great danger. It doesn't matter how profitable a business is – if it hasn't got access to adequate liquid resources, it could become insolvent (i.e. not have enough cash resources to meet its immediate liabilities). It only takes one (even very small) creditor who cannot be paid when payment is due, to petition for the company to be wound up (the equivalent of bankruptcy).

Note: this is one of the *most vital* aspects of finance of all. Managers who have a great preoccupation with 'the bottom line' may be paying attention to the wrong thing; many, many very profitable companies have gone bust simply because they have missed the importance of their cash flow and liquidity. **Cash flow and liquidity are, in fact, far more important than profitability in the short term**.

Working capital is sometimes referred to as **net liquid assets.**

The second term of importance is

Net Assets,

which is Fixed Assets *plus* Working Capital (or net liquid assets).

An alternative formula is Total Assets *minus* Current Liabilities.

You will see that either formula logically gives the same result – net assets! In effect, these are the balance of assets which are *being financed by the long-term liabilities* (in this example, the owners are the only long-term liabilities, but long-term loans would be included here where they exist).

There is a great deal of information about an organisation which can be gleaned from an understanding of the Balance Sheet and the Trading, Profit and Loss Account, as we shall see later. It is therefore very important that you really understand the layout and terms which are used.

I will finish this session with an explanation of something else which you may come across. This is a **Trial Balance**.

The Trial Balance is not part of the accounting system; it is merely a list of the net balances of every individual account. It is therefore not part of the double-entry system. Its purpose is simply to check that the totals of all the debit entries equals the totals of all the credit entries, in case single entries or incorrect figures (for one part of a double-entry) were made. To that extent, it puts all our balances 'on trial' to see if we've been guilty of a mistake in our entries. Of course, it will not tell you that something is wrong if incorrect entries were made for *both* the debit and credit aspects of a transaction.

Taking our list of accounts from the session on double-entry, before we closed the expense and sales accounts and transferred the balances to the Trading, Profit and Loss Account, the Trial Balance would have looked like this:

Trial Balance as at 15.2

	Dr	Cr
Bank	34,540	
Share Capital		100,000
Premises	50,000	
Equipment	10,000	
Business Rates	500	
Stock (Purchases)	80,000	
Creditors		45,000
Sales		69,000
Salaries and Wages	1,000	
Debtors	32,000	
Printing and Stationery	5,500	
Telephone	460	

The credits and debits each add up to the same figure – £214,000. This figure in itself is of no significance, but suggests that we have probably made correct double entries. It does not confirm that entries were made in the correct accounts, or that the figure used for each double-entry was itself correct. If we know the closing stock figure (and, for a going concern, the opening stock figure) we have all the information we need to draw up both the Trading, Profit and Loss Account and the Balance Sheet.

I will now summarise the main points from this session:

- the Balance Sheet lists all the assets and liabilities of an organisation **at one moment in time**

- it is *not* part of the double-entry system

- it is drawn up in a **vertical** format

- items are listed in reverse order of liquidity under each section

- a **fixed** asset will last longer than a normal accounting period

- a **current** asset (or current liability) is used up and replaced several times in a period

- **capital** is a long-term **liability** to the organisation

- any *undistributed* net surplus is an outstanding balance on the Trading, Profit and Loss Account and is also owed to the owners

- limited companies must show capital subscribed separately from undistributed net profit in the Balance Sheet

- the Balance Sheet *must* balance!

- it shows the total assets and how they are being funded

- it tells us how much the owners are investing in the business and in what way (capital + undistributed net profit + reserves)

- if an organisation is wound up, the owners have only the *last* claim on whatever its assets actually fetch (regardless of whatever values appear in the Balance Sheet)

- a change in value of an asset or a liability automatically leads to corresponding change(s) in other assets and/or liabilities

- there is a logical and mathematical relationship between assets, liabilities and capital

- **working capital** is a vital measure of liquidity

- a company may be highly profitable and yet be wound up if it has insufficient **liquid** resources to pay its **current** liabilities

- **net** assets are those being funded by long-term liabilities

- a Trial Balance is not an account; it is just a check that total debit entries in **all** the double-entry accounts **equal** total credit entries.

BALANCE SHEET

Exercise C – Question

Go back to the answers to Exercise A and Exercise B. Draw up the Balance Sheet as at 30.4 using the **horizontal** format. Once completed, draw it up in a **vertical** format.

BALANCE SHEET

Exercise C – Answer

Horizontal Format

Balance Sheet as at 30.4

Capital			Fixed Assets		
Original In. 80,000			Equipment	6,000	
Net Profit 1,000			Depreciation	125	
	81,000				5,875
Bank Loan	30,000		Current Assets		
		111,000	Stock	17,500	
Current Liabilities			Debtors	46,000	
Creditors		20,000	Bank	61,625	
					125,125
		131,000			131,000

Vertical format

Balance Sheets as at 30.4

	£	£
Fixed Assets		
Equipment	6,000	
Depreciation	125	
		5,875
Current Assets		
Stock	17,500	
Debtors	46,000	
Bank	61,625	
	125,125	
Current Liabilities		
Creditors	20,000	
Working Capital		105,125
Net Assets		111,000
Financed by:		
Capital	80,000	
Undistributed Net Profit	1,000	
		81,000
Bank Loan		30,000
		111,000

TRADING, PROFIT AND LOSS ACCOUNT AND BALANCE SHEET FROM TRIAL BALANCE

Exercise D – Question

From the following Trial Balance, draw up the Trading, Profit and Loss Account and Balance Sheet at the end of the year and assess the position and performance of the organisation.

Trial Balance as at 31.12

	Dr	Cr
Bank		15,500
Capital		90,000
Premises	75,000	
Motor Vehicles	36,000	
Fixtures and Fittings	15,000	
Business Rates	5,400	
Stock at 1.1	15,500	
Stock (Purchases)	112,000	
Creditors		24,500
Sales		207,300
Salaries and Wages	25,000	
Debtors	17,500	
Advertising and Display	13,500	
Administration	5,400	
Depreciation (Motor Vehicl.)	12,000	
Depreciation (Fixtures and)	5,000	

Note

Stock at 31.12 was £16,700.

TRADING, PROFIT AND LOSS ACCOUNT AND BALANCE SHEET FROM TRIAL BALANCE

Exercise D – Answer

Trading, Profit and Loss Account for the Year Ending 31.12

	%	£	£
Sales			207,300
Cost of Sales	53.45		110,800
Gross Profit	46.55		96,500
Operating Expenses			
Business Rates	2.60	5,400	
Salaries and Wages	12.06	25,000	
Advertising and Display	6.51	13,500	
Administration	2.60	5,400	
Depreciation	8.20	17,000	
			66,300
Net Profit	14.57		30,200

Note

We can calculate the cost of sales as follows:

opening stock	15,500
+ purchases	112,000
	127,500
– closing stock	16,700
Cost of Sales	110,800

Balance Sheet as at 31.12

	£	£	£
Fixed Assets			
Premises		75,000	
Motor Vehicles	48,000		
Depreciation	12,000		
		36,000	
Fixtures and Fittings	20,000		
Depreciation	5,000		
		15,000	
			126,000
Current Assets			
Stock		16,700	
Debtors		17,500	
		34,200	
Current Liabilities			
Creditors	24,500		
Bank	15,500		
		40,000	
Working Capital			(5,800)
Net Assets			120,200
Financed by:			
Share Capital		90,000	
Undistributed Net Profit		30,200	
			120,200
			120,200

Note

The bank has a *credit* balance, so we know this *must* be an overdraft!

Position and Performance

From the Trading, Profit and Loss Account, we can see that the business is very profitable. However, from the Balance Sheet we can immediately see that it has negative working capital at the end of the year. This is *extremely dangerous*, because there are insufficient *liquid* resources to pay off the creditors and overdraft.

The debtors in themselves are insufficient to pay the creditors (even assuming they pay us *before* we have to pay the creditors) and there will be a time delay before we receive payment from any new stock sales. The only way we are likely to be able to pay the creditors, therefore, is by increasing the overdraft. While the bank might be amenable to this and the overdraft may not be required to be repaid in the very short term, more liquid funds need to be injected urgently to create a positive working capital. It is not so long ago that an international bank went bust and banks have developed a poor reputation for supporting small businesses, so it is very unwise to rely on the bank facilities alone!

TRADING, PROFIT AND LOSS ACCOUNT AND BALANCE SHEET FROM TRIAL BALANCE

Exercise E – Question

From the following Trial Balance, draw up the Trading, Profit and Loss Account and Balance Sheet at the end of the year.

Trial Balance as at 5.4

	Dr	Cr
Bank	15,700	
Capital		150,000
Premises	100,000	
Motor Vehicles	60,000	
Fixtures and Fittings	16,000	
Equipment	12,000	
Business Rates	8,500	
Opening Stock	27,500	
Purchases	134,000	
Creditors		22,500
Sales		332,600
Salaries and Wages	55,000	
Debtors	37,200	
Advertising	10,300	
General Expenses	8,900	
Drawings	20,000	

Notes

1 Stock at 5.4 was £30,200.

2 All fixed assets are to be depreciated by 25 per cent.

3 Insurance has been paid in advance of the following year, to the value of £1,500.

4 Advertisements worth £2,000 were published towards the end of the period but no invoice has yet been received.

5 Some stock, which was sold for £5,000 and carried a 20 per cent margin, is to be returned unused and in perfect condition; the purchaser has not yet paid.

TRADING, PROFIT AND LOSS ACCOUNT AND BALANCE SHEET FROM TRIAL BALANCE

Exercise E – Answer

Trading, Profit and Loss Account For The Year Ending 5.4

	%	£	£
Sales			327,600
Cost of Sales	38.86		127,300
Gross Profit	61.14		200,300
Operating Expenses			
Business Rates	2.59	8,500	
Salaries and Wages	16.79	55,000	
Advertising and Display	3.75	12,300	
General Expenses	2.26	7,400	
Depreciation	14.35	47,000	
			130,200
Net Profit	21.40		70,100
Drawings			20,000
Closing Bal. c/f			50,100

Notes

1 Sales are reduced by £5,000 to reflect the sales *credit* which has not yet been made in respect of the stock to be returned.

2 We can calculate cost of sales as follows:

opening stock	27,500
+ purchases	134,000
	161,500
– closing stock	34,200
Cost of Sales	127,300

Closing stock is increased by the stock being returned *at cost value*!

3 Advertising and display are increased by £2,000; this expense was in respect of this period, but not yet entered in our accounts(which is where the Trial Balance figures came from).

4 General expenses are *reduced* by £1,500; insurance, which would be included under this heading, has been paid (and therefore entered in the account and included in the trial balance figure) in advance of the *next* trading period and should therefore be *deducted* from this year's expenses.

5 Drawings are a payment to the owners from net profit. This would be a dividend where the business is a limited company.

6 The Trading, Profit and Loss Account has a closing balance, which is carried forward – remember, this account is part of the double-entry system and so any outstanding balance is dealt within the normal way (in this case it is a liability and thus, a *credit* balance in the horizontal format). Next year, it will become the undistributed net profit balance brought forward and will be added to that year's net profit before drawings (or dividends in the case of a limited company) are deducted. This will leave next year's closing balance (which will, in turn, be carried forward).

Balance Sheet as at 5.4

	£	£	£
Fixed Assets			
Premises	100,000		
Depreciation	25,000		
		75,000	
Motor Vehicles	60,000		
Depreciation	15,000		
		45,000	
Fixtures and Fittings	16,000		
Depreciation	4,000		
		12,000	
Equipment	12,000		
Depreciation	3,000		
		9,000	
			141,000
Current Assets			
Stock		34,200	
Debtors		32,200	
Pre-paid Insurance		1,500	
Bank		15,700	
		83,600	
Current Liabilities			
Creditors	22,500		
Advertising owed	2,000		
		24,500	
Working Capital			59,100
Net Assets			200,100
Financed by:			
Capital		150,000	
Net Profit for Year	70,100		
Drawings	20,000		
Undistributed Profit		50,100	
			200,100
			200,100

Notes

1 Stock is increased to reflect the returned sale at cost value.

2 Debtors are *reduced* by £5,000, to reflect the sale return. This is done at sales value because that is the amount that debtors increased by when the original sale was made!

3 Pre-paid insurance is, in fact, a *current asset*; the insurance company *owes us* the benefit of cover in the next trading year, for which we have paid in advance.

4 We owe someone for an advertisement, which was made in the period covered by these accounts. This is therefore included in the Balance Sheet as a *current liability*.

5 Net profit for the year is *reduced* by the drawings, to show how much undistributed profit is carried forward to the start of the next year. If there had been any undistributed profit brought forward, this would have been *added* into the calculations.

Session 5
••
Do we understand what's going on?

☞ *Ask:* given what you now know about financial information and where it comes from, what useful information could you glean from the Trading, Profit and Loss Account and Balance Sheet of an organisation?

Answer: how much net profit is made. What the gross profit margin is. What the operating expenses are, both in absolute terms and as a percentage to sales. What assets and liabilities exist as at the Balance Sheet date. How much working capital is available and whether there are enough liquid funds to pay the current liabilities. What the net assets are and how they are being funded; in particular, how much the owners have invested.

As we can see, there is already a great deal of vital information available to us, now that we understand where the figures come from and what they can tell us about the organisation. So far, however, we have concentrated on the layout and content of the final accounts (the Trading, Profit and Loss Account or equivalent) and Balance Sheet. If we look a bit deeper, we will be able to find out even more about what is going on and where the organisation may be heading. We are therefore going to consider the information from these documents further.

THE BOTTOM LINE

Have you ever heard a newsreader announce in very emotive terms that 'such and such a company' increased its profits last year by £50 million? Or that a company's sales have increased by 25 per cent? I have – often, along with the opposite situations.

☞ *Ask:* when you hear this, what does it tell you?

Answer: nothing! First of all, can you visualise or appreciate £50 million? Even if you are fortunate enough to be able to, it still tells you precisely nothing! Oh, the 'man in the street' will complain that such a huge profit is obscene; why should *they* pay higher bills to enlarge the huge profits of this corporation? The fact is, if it was such a significant profit, we would all be clamber-ing to buy the shares of the company in question, because then that huge profit would come to us! Of course, there isn't usually a great queue of people rushing to buy the shares.

Another favourite with the newscasters is how much profit BT is making every minute. Again, though, this is a completely meaningless figure. The problem is,the newscasters are usually financially less aware than you already are.

Let's consider two Trading, Profit and Loss Account 'bottom line' figures.Let's say that Company A makes a net profit for the year of £5 million and that Company B makes a net profit for the same year of £10 million pounds.

Ask: if you had £10,000 to invest, which company's shares would you buy? *Answer:* I don't know! I simply haven't got enough information! For instance, how much money was invested in each business in order to earn their net profits? It could be, for example, that Company B actually had net assets which are ten times higher than Company A, yet only produced twice the net profit. It could be that Company B is so illiquid that it will soon be forced into receivership. It could be that Company B's profits are declining, whereas Company A's are rising steeply. We don't know the **price** of the shares – they may be at a large **premium** to the net asset value of the company – or how many have been issued. Suppose we are interested in **income** rather than **cap-ital growth** for our investment; perhaps Company B retains most of its net profit for **reinvestment**, whereas Company A pays most of its net profit out in the form of **dividends**!

I could go on. However, I think you can see just how misleading and danger-ous it is to react to figures without really understanding what you're looking at, what it tells you and what other information you need, for it to be mean-ingful and useful.

The more we can understand the financial relationships which exist, the better will be our position when making judgements and decisions. So let's take another look at the Trading, Profit and Loss Account which we have drawn up from our original set of transactions:

Trading, Profit and Loss Account for the Period 1.1 – 15.2

	%	£	£
Sales			69,000
Cost of Sales	85.51		59,000
Gross Profit	14.49		10,000
Operating Expenses			
Business Rates	0.72	500	
Salaries and Wages	1.45	1,000	
Printing and Stationery	7.97	5,500	
Telephone	0.67	460	
			7,460
Net Profit			2,540

☞ *Ask:* which of these figures are 100 per cent accurate?
Answer: sales; business rates; salaries and wages; printing and stationery; telephone. Cost of sales is not accurate – it is an estimate.

☞ *Ask:* why?
Answer: because we can never be absolutely certain of the value of our closing stock. Apart from assessing its real value, we can rarely count and check every item – even when doing a stock-take. This means that our opening and closing stock figures are estimates. If our opening and closing stock figures are estimates, then our cost of sales figure must also be an estimate, since we used these figures together with purchases (which is an accurate figure) to calculate it. This means, in turn, that the gross profit and, therefore, the net profit figure must be estimates too.

Another item which usually appears but which is not accurate is **depreciation**. Once more, this can only ever be an estimate (until the relevant asset is sold – even then, we wouldn't know how much of the loss in value since its purchase was derived from a particular year, assuming it had been held for more than one). As an operating expense, depreciation would also reduce the accuracy of the net profit figure. Let's have another look at the Balance Sheet:

Balance Sheet as at 15.2

	£	£
Fixed Assets		
Premises	50,000	
Equipment	10,000	
		60,000
Current Assets		
Stock	21,000	
Debtors	32,000	
Bank	34,540	
	87,540	
Current Liabilities		
Creditors	45,000	
Working Capital		42,540
Net Assets		102,540
Financed by:		
Share Capital	100,000	
Undistributed Net Profit	2,540	
		102,540
		102,540

Ask: are there figures *here* which are only estimates?

Answer: yes; premises, equipment and stock. As a result of these figures being only estimates, working capital, net assets and the long-term ownership interest are also inaccurate. They are all based on imperfect information.

This means that not only do we not always *use* the information available to us, but even when we do we are building on a foundation of *estimates* and *assumptions*. Our conclusions, no matter how rigorously derived, will only be as good as those estimates and assumptions. This is one of the main reasons why professional bodies *insist* on particular accounting standards.

A typical take-over bid might occur where the asset values shown in an organisation's Balance Sheet are out of date – especially in times of high inflation. Where this happens, the company's share price will be lower because the assets are undervalued. When the bidder realises this and is successful in taking over the company, assets and parts of the business might be sold for much more than the values shown in the books. The film 'Other People's Money' illustrates such a situation!

So, now we know; even that most sacred cow, The Bottom Line, is an illusory figure! However, enough of what we don't know – let's turn our attention to what we can find out.

Return on investment

☞ *Ask:* if a friend suggested that you should make an investment, what is the first thing you would be interested in knowing?

Answer: how safe is it?

Ask: what next?

Answer: how much are we likely to make? Generally with investment, there is a **risk-reward relationship**. This means that people are willing to increase their **risk** as they increase their potential **reward**, or return. That is quite logical; each individual will have their own level of acceptance of risk based on this relationship. Therefore, we need to establish two things; the return and the risk. Let's look at the return side of the relationship first.

We need to calculate what **rate of return** is being achieved by the company in question. With the information from the Trading, Profit and Loss Account and the Balance Sheet, we *have* this information. Our **return** will be the net profit for the year (whether distributed or not).We need to divide this return by the **capital employed** in the business during the period when it arose. The capital employed can be defined in various ways, so we must always go back to rule number one – when someone supplies a **Rate of Return on Capital Employed** (sometimes known as ROCE), we *must* check what figures have been used so that we fully *understand* what we are looking at!

Using our example, the only long-term capital employed is that attributable to the owners. The figure here is the same as the figure for net assets. However, there is one slight difficulty if we want to get the best possible estimate of our rate of return. The problem is, we have ended up with *more* capital employed at the end of the year than at the start! This is due to the net profit element which has been accumulating during the period – like the interest in a building society account. It would be unfair to accept capital employed as including all of the profit (which was not invested originally by the owners). On the other hand, while the accumulating net profit remains *in* the business it is *adding* to the capital employed at the start of the period. In order to adjust for this, we add the **opening capital employed** to the **closing capital employed** and then divide by two. This gives us an **average capital employed** for the period.

Let's look at our example. At the start, our capital employed was £100,000. At the end, it was £102,540 (original capital invested plus undistributed net profit). This is what we do:

$$\frac{100,000 + 102,540}{2} = 101,270$$

Net profit for the period (whether distributed or not) was £2,540. So we can now calculate our return on average capital employed:

$$\frac{2,540}{101,270} \times 100 = 2.51\%$$

This is a *very* revealing figure, since it can be used to compare against other potential investments or companies' performances. In effect, it means simply that this company has made a return on its investment of 2.51 per cent *over a six week period*; remember, the transactions upon which the Trading, Profit and Loss Account were based took place between 2 January and 15 February! This calculation provides one of the most interesting and important figures available to us – far more valuable than net profit.

I mentioned that there are other ways of calculating this important measure. For instance, **total** assets are sometimes used for **capital employed**. Complications also arise when part of the long-term funding is provided by someone other than the owners, e.g. a long-term fixed-interest loan. In this case, a decision must be made as to whether to include the loan in calculating the capital employed. If we *exclude* it, we will be identifying the capital employed attributable to the owners. If we *include* it, we may need to add back to the net profit the interest paid for the loan in the period, since this also is part of the return on *that* capital employed!

We shall keep things simple here, but *do* check the *basis* on which such figures are worked out when you come across them.

Now that we have examined the reward, we should also consider the **risk**. In order to do this, when assessing an investment in a company we would want to ask lots of questions about its management, products, plans and past performance. As we saw in a previous session, however, a company can be extremely profitable and yet be insolvent. An examination of the Balance Sheet will provide information which can tell us how safe our money would be as far as liquidity is concerned.

Liquidity

☞ *Ask:* what is working capital?

Answer: current assets minus current liabilities. So, in fact, we already know of one important measure of liquidity which we can use to assess a company's position. This measure is sometimes called the **current ratio**. How high the ratio needs to be depends on a number of factors, but clearly it needs to be much higher than 1 and probably higher than 2 in most situations (2 would mean that there are twice as many current assets as current liabilities; this may be expressed as 2:1).

☞ *Ask:* what makes up current assets?

Answer: stock, debtors, cash. It is all very well saying that these things need to be enough to pay off all our current liabilities, but stock may not easily, or (more importantly) *quickly*, be turned into cash to pay the liabilities. It is therefore useful to look at a ratio of liquid assets to current liabilities. The **quick ratio** should normally be higher than 1, or we may be in great danger. This is the calculation:

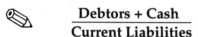

$$\frac{\textbf{Debtors + Cash}}{\textbf{Current Liabilities}}$$

Even with the quick ratio, however, we are assuming that all our debtors pay on time and do not default. Although we must ensure that we have sufficient liquid resources, we also do not want too much, because of another characteristic of investment. This is that, generally, money which is invested in a liqued form earns a lower rate of return than money which is not. To prove this point, just think of building societies; they pay a higher rate of interest on money that is invested for a set period e.g. ninety days. If our liquidity ratios are very high, therefore, it could be that the organisation is not using its resources very efficiently.

Turning to our worked example, we can calculate the liquidity ratios. To do this, we will take the following information from the balance sheet:

Current Assets

Stock	21,000
Debtors	32,000
Bank	34,540
	87,540

Current Liabilities

Creditors	45,000

The current ratio is:

$$\frac{87,540}{45,000} = 1.95$$

The quick ratio is:

$$\frac{66,540}{45,000} = 1.48$$

These would suggest that the company is in quite a healthy position.

What we are now doing is analysing the performance and position of an organisation by using ratios to measure particular aspects. There is one very important point I must make with regard to calculating ratios. When presented with a set of published accounts, or an annual report, there is a great deal of important information to be found in the **notes**, which usually take up many more pages than the accounts themselves. For some of the information which you need to calculate the ratios (or to decide what version of a ratio to use) you will have to look there.

There are as many ratios which can be used as there is imagination and creativity of the users, but we will consider a few more very important ones.

Margin and mark-up

One important figure from our Trading, Profit and Loss Account is the **gross profit margin**. This is defined as gross profit as a percentage of sales. We therefore carry out the following calculation:

$$\frac{\textbf{Gross Profit}}{\textbf{Sales}} \times 100$$

Using our worked example, the appropriate figures are:

$$\frac{10,000}{69,000} \times 100 = 14.49\%$$

In fact, we worked this out when we calculated the percentage column in the vertical Trading, Profit and Loss Account. Conversely, the cost of sales was 85.51 per cent of sales:

$$\frac{59{,}000}{69{,}000} \times 100$$

or 100% − 14.49%

In this example, we have two ways of calculating a figure. This brings us to a very important key point:

Where there is more than one way to find a figure, do it both ways.

This gives us absolute confidence that our figure *must* be correct. It is all too easy to come up with a wrong figure, in which case not only is our later interpretation faulty but so are subsequent calculations based on that figure. Wrong information is worse than no information.

Now we will deal with something which can cause problems later on. In essence, it is quite straightforward. If we know that sales are marked down by the gross profit percentage to arrive back at **cost of sales** (*Note*: make *sure* they see the logic of this), then we can work back from the other way. In other words, we can apply a percentage to **cost of sales** and *add* the resulting figure in order to arrive back at Sales. This percentage is called the **mark-up**, and it carries a set relationship with the **margin**. Let's look at the way we can calculate it:

$$\frac{\text{Gross Profit}}{\text{Cost of Sales}} \times 100$$

Using the figures in our Trading, Profit and Loss Account, we can work out the mark-up for our example company:

$$\frac{10{,}000}{59{,}000} \times 100 = 16.95\%$$

In other words, if we take stock at purchase cost (allowing for damages and theft) and *add* the mark-up at 16.95 per cent, we will arrive at its sales value. I mentioned that margin and mark-up have a set relationship. This can be demonstrated by Fig. 5.1.

This is a very, very useful tool to bear in mind. Every time you get confused about mark-up, margin or other breakdowns of sales into the constituent parts, re-draw the illustration of margin and mark-up, put the actual figures in and *make sure you understand the underlying relationships!*

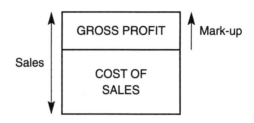

Fig. 5.1 Margin and Mark-up

From the diagram, you will see that gross profit is the same in *actual* terms as the mark-up; the difference comes because of what the profit element is compared *to* (in percentage terms). It is compared with sales to calculate the margin – going *down* to cost of sales. It is compared with cost of sales to mark them *up* to sales. Further, there is a mathematical way of converting one to the other:

Step 1

Convert the percentage (mark-up or margin) to a fraction by putting it over 100. Using the gross profit margin for our example company, the percentage Margin of 14.49 per cent is converted to the following fraction:

$$\frac{14.49}{100}$$

Step 2

We now change the value of the fraction. Whether we are going from margin to mark-up or from mark-up to margin, *the top figure in the fraction remains the same*. In this case, it will be 14.49. The only thing that we must decide is whether we add or subtract the top figure to or from the lower figure to get the new lower figure.

It is very helpful to remember the **logic** at this point; mark-up is *always* going to be a *higher* figure **as a percentage** than margin, since it is the same amount but as a proportion of a smaller figure (cost of sales should be lower than sales). If our percentage is to end up *higher*, therefore, we must *subtract* the top figure in order to arrive at the right fraction. If we were going from mark-up to margin, we would *add* the top figure to the bottom figure. This is all you need to remember. So, if we take our margin of 14.49 per cent, we can calculate the mark-up thus:

$$\frac{14.49}{100} \text{ (the margin) changes to } \frac{14.49}{85.51} \text{ (the mark-up)}$$

Step 3

The only thing left to do is to convert the new fraction back to a percentage. We do this simply by dividing the top number by the bottom number and multiplying the result by 100.

$$\frac{14.49}{85.51} \times 100 = 16.95\%$$

Again, we have confirmed our earlier calculation using a different method, so we know the figure *must* be correct. If you ever get confused, draw the diagram and put in simple figures to check that you understand these relationships.

Note: the understanding of the relationships between sales, cost of sales, mark-up and margin is crucial. Further breakdowns and new terminology will be used later, so make absolutely certain that they (and you) fully understand what has just been covered.

We have looked at the most recent **returns** produced by an organisation and considered the **risk**. We can also look at some aspects of **efficiency**.

Turnover ratios

We shall consider three very important **turnover** ratios. These relate to the average stock, debtors and creditors and we can calculate the ratio for each. Turnover means the number of times in a period that the average stock/debtors/creditors (according to which ratio we are considering) is used up and replaced. From what we already know, therefore, these ratios are all concerned with *current* assets or liabilities. Let's consider each one in turn.

 Ask: how do debtors arise?
Answer: from sales. In order to calculate any turnover ratio, we need two pieces of information which have a logical relationship. This is very important, because it will help you remember how to work something out without relying on finding 'the formula'. In fact, I am going to emphasise this point generally. If people rely on a list of formulae, they:

(**a**) use the wrong one
(**b**) don't recognise a completely *wrong* answer because they are relying on their list rather than their own understanding and logic
(**c**) are confused if presented with a question from a different perspective to that from which their formulae are presented
(**d**) are utterly lost if the formula they need isn't on their list.

Believe me, it's true! So we will try to always understand the *logic* rather than just taking and using 'the formula'.

Now, we have said that debtors arise because of sales. Debtors are people who owe us money; hopefully, they will pay up within a short period of time and be replaced by new ones as we continue making sales. If we take total sales for the period and divide the average number of debtors which exist at any one moment in time, we can see how many times during the period *average* debtors have been replaced, or 'turned over'. This is our **debtor turnover rate**.

From a different starting point, the logic is that each time we replace the debtors, we are adding to the total sales figure for the period; if we were to multiply the *number of times* we replace them in a period by the average that exist at any one time, we must arrive at the total sales figure for that period. This is assuming, of course, that *all* sales are made on *credit* – otherwise an adjustment must be made to take out the cash sales from our calculations.

Going back to our working example, we have the necessary figures to calculate the debtor turnover rate. However, we must bear in mind that this business has only traded for six weeks and so our figures would not be as useful as for a full year in respect of a going concern. The principle and means of calculation are similar, though. We need two pieces of information – sales and average debtors. From our Balance Sheet as at 15.2 (the end of the period) we know that debtors were valued at £32,000. To obtain average debtors, we need to add this figure to our debtors at the start (in this case £0) and divide by 2. Of course, this is a very rough and ready average – especially since we are just starting the business. Even in a full year where the company *has* been trading previously, this average could easily be distorted if just one of these figures is a little misleading; this could happen, for example, if the business had made an unusually large sale just before the Balance Sheet date. In the real world, therefore, we would take the figures for debtors on a much more regular basis – every month for a year and divide by 12, or every week and divide by 52. Naturally, we would have to take these figures at *regular* intervals. The better the average we can use, the more accurate the turnover rate will be. This applies to the other turnover rates as well.

We can obtain the sales figure from the Trading, Profit and Loss Account. We said a short while ago, however, that the debtor turnover rate should only include sales which were made on credit and not for cash (no debtors arise on a cash sale!). If we go back to the individual accounts in our working example, we find that £15,000 of sales were made in exchange for cash. As a result, we must adjust our sales figure of £69,000 by deducting £15,000; the remaining figure of £54,000 is derived purely from *credit* sales and is therefore the one we use to calculate debtor turnover. In our example, credit sales divided by average debtors is:

$$\frac{54{,}000}{16{,}000} = 3.37$$

This means, in effect, that the average debtors are replaced 3.37 times in this period. Since we know that this period is made up of six weeks, we can divide the number of days (45) by the rate to give us the number of days on average that it takes for our debtors to pay us:

$$\frac{45}{3.37} = 13 \text{ days}$$

If the period was a full year, we would simply divide 365 by the debtor turnover rate for the year to tell us how many days (on average) our debtors take to pay. Here, to establish our annual rate, we would divide 365 days by 45 days, then multiply the result by the rate for the 45-day period. Using the 45-day rate at its most accurate level (three decimal places = 3.375) we would end up with an annual rate of 27.37. Dividing this rate into 365 returns us to 13 days; we know that we have done the calculations correctly because this is the same number of days as for a shorter trading period.

Ask: what is the importance of knowing how many days it takes for debtors to pay?
Answer: the sooner we can get our money, the better! It is part of our working capital and we need it to pay off our creditors in due course.

Let's look at another turnover ratio. Creditors are, in effect, the other side of the coin. If we can delay payment it will help our cashflow, giving us longer to get our debtors to pay up. Besides, if we can use this money we will need less of our own. We may as well keep the money earning interest for as long as possible; it all adds to our Net Profit at the end of the year. In fact, many small suppliers have literally been squeezed to death by negative cashflow when large organisations have taken months to pay them, causing fatal liquidity problems. After all, large companies expect to be paid promptly even when they are awful payers themselves.

Ask: how do creditors arise?
Answer: through *purchases*. So, the two figures we need in order to calculate

the **creditor turnover** rate are purchases and average creditors. From our Stock Account, we calculated purchases to be £80,000. Once again, in our example, creditors at the start date were £0; at the end they were valued at £45,000.Average creditors during the period were therefore £22,500 and our credit or turnover rate will be:

$$\frac{80,000}{22,500} = 3.56$$

Forty-five (days) divided by this rate gives 13 days; this is how long we took, on average, to pay the people we owe money to for stock which we purchased. Compared with the debtor turnover rate for the same period, it shows that we are collecting the money from credit transactions at about the same time we are paying it out! We would be interested in improving this situation if possible by taking *longer* to pay our creditors than it takes to collect the debts due to us. In a normal situation, once the business is established, we could certainly expect to take longer to pay our creditors but would probably have to *extend* credit for longer to our (increasingly trusted) customers!

There is one other turnover rate which we will consider. Cost of sales is, in effect, sales at cost value. If we divide this figure by average stock, we will establish our **stock turnover rate**. In our example, stock at the start is £0; at 15.2 it is £21,000. Average stock was therefore £10,500, so our stock turnover rate will be:

$$\frac{59,000}{10,500} = 5.62$$

In other words, we replaced our stock every eight days.

Ask: why is this figure significant?
Answer: because the more times we turn our stock over, the more money we will make. For instance, let's suppose that our sales include a 5 per cent gross profit margin. For every £100 of sales, we are left with £5. If our stockturn rate is 5, we have made a Gross Profit for the period of £25. If, however, our turnover rate drops to 4, our Gross Profit will drop by 20 per cent, to £20.

Note: make sure that everyone can see the importance and value of the turnover ratios (and the value of *percentages* as opposed to absolute figures).

Gearing ratios

You may have heard about companies getting into trouble because they are highly geared. **Gearing** is very important and deserves explanation, because it can have a dramatic effect on the fortunes of a company. Basically, gearing is the degree to which an organisation employs fixed interest as opposed to owners' capital funding, although there are (like capital employed) various ways of defining it. We shall consider two ways in particular (but I will mention a third). Let's look at the Balance Sheet we drew up for Exercise C:

Balance Sheet as at 30.4

	£	£
Fixed Assets		
Equipment	6,000	
Depreciation	125	
		5,875
Current Assets		
Stock	17,500	
Debtors	46,000	
Bank	61,625	
	125,125	
Current Liabilities		
Creditors	20,000	
Working Capital		105,125
Net Assets		111,000
Financed by:		
Capital	80,000	
Undistributed Net Profit	1,000	
		81,000
Bank Loan		30,000
		111,000

Let's look at how this organisation is being financed.

Ask: how much capital is attributable to the owners?
Answer: £81,000. That leaves the £30,000 which is being borrowed from the bank. On paper, the business is worth £111,000 – that is the value of its net assets. Since £30,000 is being funded with borrowed money, the **gearing ratio** is:

$$\frac{30,000}{111,000} = 0.27$$

If we assume, however, that the return on capital employed is 30 per cent and the rate of interest charged on the loan is only 20 per cent, the owners are, in effect, earning an overall profit by employing the bank's money. The problem (and danger) is that a company will borrow even more under these circumstances, so that its gearing increases to a very high level. If a recession comes and/or interest rates rise, the return on capital employed might fall and the burden of debt could force a major crisis. At the very least in this situation, the trading position would be severely weakened at the worst possible time and the cost of the loan would drain the organisation of funds.

It can be seen that gearing is very worthwhile when things are going well, but all businesses face downturns on a cyclical basis and do not want to be highly geared when this happens. If they are, the risks which we considered earlier would dramatically increase. Gearing is therefore something which we should look at when analysing a business.

The second way of measuring gearing is by dividing the fixed interest funding by the owners' funds (as opposed to net assets, as we did on the first basis). This gives us a higher ratio:

$$\frac{30,000}{81,000} = 0.37$$

I said I would mention a third method of calculating gearing. Although the book value of the company is its net assets figure, its market value may be quite different. Often it could be higher, but sometimes it will be lower. This will depend on all sorts of factors, such us the demand and supply for the company's shares, stock market sentiment generally, the fact that the business is a 'going concern', future growth prospects and so on. In any case, it is possible to divide the fixed interest funding into the market value of the company. This gives our third method of calculating gearing.

You may be asking (if you haven't already) how we know whether the ratios which we end up with are good or bad. This will depend on the whole situation. It is very important to realise that:

financial analysis is more likely to tell you what questions to ask rather than provide the answers.

This means that the reasons for certain ratio figures could often be due to quite opposing possible explanations. For example, let's suppose that our stockturn rate drops to 15 from 10. On the face of it, this is bad because it results in less Gross Profit. However, it *might* be good! Perhaps we have raised our gross profit margins, so that we sell our stock less often but make more profit every time we do. Maybe we're 'stocking up' at the end of the year (resulting in a high closing stock figure and thus reducing our stockturn ratio) in anticipation of an expansion in sales in the following period. Think of a supermarket; it may operate on very small gross margins, yet turn its stock over several times a week. A jeweller, on the other hand, may have enormous margins but only turn his stock over two or three times a year. Apart from this, the Gross Profit margin which we have calculated assumes an average margin for all products sold. In fact, sales will be made up of many different products, carrying different margins, with different quantities sold in each case. In other words, changing our product mix has a part to play as well.

Remember where we started; one or two facts, figures or ratios tell us nothing in themselves. What we really need to do is compare this year's figures with others from:

1 this year;
2 previous years;
3 our competitors;
4 our *planned* figures.

We should therefore follow this procedure:

(a) Number crunch first, as much as possible.
(b) Interpret *afterwards*, but don't jump to conclusions – ask further questions.

I will now summarise the main points from this session:

- we can glean a great deal of information about the performance and position of an organisation through an analysis of its Trading, Profit and Loss Account and Balance Sheets

- *isolated* figures tell you nothing and *could* be very misleading

- *don't* jump to conclusions

- *don't* get mesmerised by 'the bottom line'

- some values in the Trading, Profit and Loss Account and Balance Sheet (*including* net profit) are 'best estimates' based on assumptions

- that is why published accounts and reports must conform to *accounting standards*

- various ratios can help assess an organisation's **rewards, risks** and **efficiency**

- when working out ratios, check by working them out in more than one way, where possible

- when presented with ratios, check that you understand the *basis* on which they were calculated

- it is particularly important to understand and remember the relationships between *margin, mark-up* and *sales*

- don't rely on lists of formulae – use **logic**

- use ratios to **compare** with other figures and establish areas which need investigation.

Note: the following exercises may best be used by having them completed in syndicates, where it is the trainees' responsibility in each syndicate not just to get the right answers, but also to make sure *everyone* understands how answers were derived and agrees that they are correct.

ACCOUNTING RATIOS

Exercise F – Question

1 Using the answers to exercises D and E, calculate the following:

(a) margin
(b) mark-up
(c) net profit margin
(d) the return on capital employed
(e) working capital ratio
(f) quick ratio
(g) average stockturn and the number of days stock is held on average
(h) average debtor turnover and number of days debtors take to pay on average
(j) average creditor turnover and the number of days taken to pay creditors on average

Note

Assume that all stock purchases and sales were made on a credit basis and that the figures in the Balance Sheets at the start of the year were as follows:

	Exercise D	Exercise E
Debtors	£18,500	£30,800
Creditors	£3,500	£7,500

2 Compare the results of your analysis of the two companies and assess (a) their relative performance, (b) the degree of risks they run and (c) their efficiency.

ACCOUNTING RATIOS

Exercise F – Answer

1 Accounting ratio calculations

(a) Margin

Exercise D

$$\frac{96,500}{207,300} \times 100 = \textbf{46.55\%}$$

Exercise E

$$\frac{200,300}{327,600} \times 100 = \textbf{61.14\%}$$

(b) mark-up

$$\frac{96,500}{110,800} \times 100 = \textbf{87.09\%}$$

$$\frac{200,300}{127,300} \times 100 = \textbf{157.34\%}$$

or

$$\frac{46.55}{53.45} \times 100 = \textbf{87.09\%}$$

$$\frac{61.14}{38.86} \times 100 = \textbf{157.33\%}$$

(c) net profit margin

$$\frac{30,200}{207,300} \times 100 = \textbf{14.57\%}$$

$$\frac{70,100}{327,600} \times 100 = \textbf{21.40\%}$$

(d) the return on capital employed

average capital employed:

$$\frac{90,000 + 120,200}{2} = 105,100$$

$$\frac{150,000 + 200,100}{2} = 175,050$$

the return:

$$\frac{30,200}{105,100} \times 100 = \textbf{28.73\%}$$

$$\frac{70,100}{175,050} \times 100 = \textbf{40.05\%}$$

(e) working capital ratio

$$\frac{34,200}{40,000} = \textbf{0.85}$$

$$\frac{83,600}{24,500} = \textbf{3.41}$$

(f) quick ratio

Exercise D	**Exercise E**
$\dfrac{17,500}{40,000} = \mathbf{0.44}$	$\dfrac{47,900}{24,500} = \mathbf{1.95}$

(g) average stockturn

average stock:

$$\frac{15,500 + 16,700}{2} = 16,100 \qquad \frac{27,500 + 34,200}{2} = 30,850$$

rate:

$$\frac{110,800}{16,100} = \mathbf{6.88} \qquad \frac{127,300}{30,850} = \mathbf{4.13}$$

time stock is held on average:

$$\frac{365}{6.88} = \mathbf{53\ days} \qquad \frac{365}{4.13} = \mathbf{88\ days}$$

(h) average debtor turnover

average debtors:

$$\frac{18,500 + 17,500}{2} = 18,000 \qquad \frac{30,800 + 32,200}{2} = 31,500$$

rate:

$$\frac{207,300}{18,000} = \mathbf{11.52} \qquad \frac{327,600}{31,500} = \mathbf{10.40}$$

time taken to collect debts:

$$\frac{365}{11.52} = \mathbf{32\ days} \qquad \frac{365}{10.4} = \mathbf{35\ days}$$

(j) average creditor turnover

average creditors:

$$\frac{3,500 + 24,500}{2} = 14,000 \qquad \frac{7,500 + 22,500}{2} = 15,000$$

rate:

$$\frac{112,000}{14,000} = 8$$

$$\frac{134,000}{15,000} = 8.93$$

time taken to pay debts:

$$\frac{365}{8} = 46 \text{ days}$$

$$\frac{365}{8.93} = 41 \text{ days}$$

2(a) Relative performance

The company in Exercise E clearly produces a much better return. Its gross profit margin is much higher than that of the company in Exercise D; its net profit margin is 47 per cent higher. Even more significantly, in Exercise E the return on capital employed is 39 per cent higher – a *much* better return for the people who have invested their money in this business.

2(b) Relative risk

Once again, the company in Exercise E comes out much better, with a very healthy liquidity situation. The company in Exercise D has no *immediate* cash resources; it is effectively living off its bank overdraft. The value of its creditors exceeds the debtors value, which implies that the bank overdraft will have to increase. Let's hope that the goodwill of the bank can be relied on and that this company has an agreed facility well in excess of the current level! After all, the owners *are* receiving a reasonable rate of return on their investment and so it would be a pity if the business was forced into liquidation.

2(c) Relative efficiency

Both companies are operating quite efficiently to the extent that they are collecting their debts sooner than they are paying their creditors – especially with the company in Exercise D. Here, the company collects 43 per cent sooner than it pays (as opposed to 17 per cent faster in the case of the Exercise E company). In both cases, however, the reason why creditors have increased so substantially over the year would have to be investigated – particularly when stock levels have only slightly increased (especially with the Exercise D example). It *might* be because the companies are taking longer to pay the creditors at the end of the year than at the start, so that at any one time the amount owed is higher.

The company in Exercise D turns its stock over *much* faster than the company in Exercise E. It would be interesting to see whether they sell similar products.

However, the margin on which the Exercise E company operates is much higher, so it is not too unexpected that it will have a lower stockturn. We can see who makes the better return on stock handling and margins:

	Company D	*Company E*
gross profit per £100 average stock at sales value	£46.55	£61.14
× stockturn	6.88	4.13
	£320.26	£252.51

The resulting figures represent the gross profit earned on every £100 of average stock at sales value over the year as a whole. This is because when stock is valued at sales value, we have calculated the gross profit in total by multiplying how many times we turn it over by the gross profit we make each time.

If the companies did sell similar products, it is clear that on this basis the company in Exercise D is actually more efficient in its sales and marketing operation. It is also interesting in this scenario to add up the relative operating costs of the two companies as a percentage of sales; here again, the Exercise D company comes out significantly better (31.97% compared with 39.74%). On this basis, the company would do much better if it increased its sales through expansion. This would necessitate holding higher stock levels and would assume that it would be possible to sell a lot more – not an unreasonable assumption, since its rival is already selling more at higher margins. However, the Exercise D company is in a dangerous situation, with inadequate working capital for its existing level of operation. It needs a significant injection of working capital and would need more still if it was going to carry higher stocks in order to sell more.

The end result of all this is that in Exercise D, the business was unable to pay drawings or a dividend – it urgently needed its net profit to reduce its overdraft. Its rival, however, was able to pay an income to the owners because of its healthy working capital position.

DOUBLE-ENTRY BOOKKEEPING; TRADING PROFIT AND LOSS ACCOUNT AND BALANCE SHEET

Exercise G – Question

1 Enter the following events in the individual accounts of a new business and then balance off the accounts, drawing up the Trading, Profit and Loss Account and Balance Sheet as at 15 February.

2.1   Business started with £100,000 in cash
2.1   Bank loan obtained for £20,000
5.1   £3,000 paid for rent and business rates for the period
10.1 Goods bought for £45,000 on credit from R. Jones Ltd
15.1 Office equipment purchased for £10,000 in cash
20.1 Goods sold to M. Smith for a £25,000 cheque
25.1 Van purchased for £10,000 in cash
31.1 Goods sold for £40,000 on credit to K. Irving
5.2   Cheque for £45,000 paid to R. Jones Ltd
6.2   Bank interest of £350 paid in cash in respect of loan
9.2   Goods bought on credit from R. May Ltd. for £60,000
15.2 Closing stocks were valued at £45,000
15.2 Depreciation on the van for the period was £125
15.2 Depreciation on office equipment for the period was £125

2 Analyse the accounts to establish the following ratios:

(**a**) margin
(**b**) mark-up
(**c**) net profit margin
(**d**) the return on capital employed attributable to the owner
(**e**) the return on capital employed (including the loan)
(**f**) working capital ratio
(**g**) quick ratio
(**h**) gearing (to owner's capital)
(**i**) gearing (to net assets)
(**j**) average stockturn and the number of days stock is held on average
(**k**) average debtor turnover and number of days debtors take to pay on average
(**l**) average creditor turnover and the number of days taken to pay creditors on average.

DOUBLE-ENTRY BOOKKEEPING; TRADING PROFIT AND LOSS ACCOUNT AND BALANCE SHEET

Exercise G – Answer

1 Events entered in relevant accounts

Capital Account

15.2	Closing Bal. c/f	100,000	2.1	Initial Investment	100,000
		100,000			100,000
			16.2	Opening Bal. b/f	100,000

Bank Account

2.1	Initial Investment – C.	100,000	5.1	Rent and Business	3,000
2.1	Loan – Bank Loan	20,000	15.1	Purchase – Office	10,000
20.1	M. Smith – Sales	25,000	25.1	Purchase – Van	10,000
			5.2	R. Jones Ltd – C.	45,000
			6.2	Interest – Bank	350
			16.2	Closing Bal. c/f	76,650
		145,000			145,000
16.2	Opening Bal. b/f	76,650			

Bank Loan Account

15.2	Closing Bal. c/f	20,000	2.1	Loan – Bank	20,000
		20,000			20,000
			16.2	Opening Bal. b/f	20,000

Rent and Business Rates Account

5.1	Rent and Business Rates	3,000	15.2	Closing Bal. – T.	3,000
		3,000			3,000

Stock Account

10.1	R. Jones Ltd – Creditors	45,000	15.2 Closing Stock c.	45,000
9.2	R. May Ltd – Creditors	60,000	15.2 Cost of Goods S.	60,000
		105,000		105,000
16.2	Opening Stock b/f	45,000		

Creditors Account

5.2	R. Jones Ltd. – Bank	45,000	10.1 R. Jones Ltd –	45,000
15.2	Closing Bal. c/f	60,000	9.2 R. May Ltd – St.	60,000
		105,000		105,000
			16.2 Opening Bal. b/f	60,000

Office Equipment Account

15.1	Purchase – Bank	10,000	15.2 Depreciation – D.	125
			15.2 Closing Bal. c/f	9,875
		10,000		10,000
16.2	Opening Bal. b/f	9,875		

Sales Account

15.2	Closing Bal. – Trading,	65,000	20.1 M. Smith – Bank	25,000
			31.1 K. Irving – Debt.	40,000
		65,000		65,000

Van Account

25.1	Purchase – Bank	10,000	15.2 Depreciation – D.	125
			15.2 Closing Bal. c/f	9,875
		10,000		10,000
16.2	Opening Bal. b/f	9,875		

Debtors Account

31.1 K. Irving – Sales	40,000	15.2 Closing Bal. c/f	40,000
	40,000		40,000
16.2 Opening Bal. b/f	40,000		

Bank Interest Account

6.2 Loan Interest – Bank	350	15.2 Closing Bal. – T.	350
	350		350

Depreciation Account

15.2 Depreciation – Van	125	15.2 Closing Bal. – T.	250
15.2 Depreciation – Office	125		
	250		250

Trading, Profit and Loss Account for the Period 2.1 – 15.2

	%	£	£
Sales			65,000
Cost of Sales	92.31		60,000
Gross Profit	7.69		5,000
Operating Expenses			
Rent and Business Rates	4.62	3,000	
Bank Interest	0.54	350	
Depreciation	0.38	250	
			3,600
Net Profit	2.15		1,400

Balance Sheet as at 15.2

	£	£	£
Fixed Assets			
Office Equipment	10,000		
Depreciation	125		
		9,875	
Van	10,000		
Depreciation	125		
		9,875	
			19,750
Current Assets			
Stock		45,000	
Debtors		40,000	
Bank		76,650	
		161,650	
Current Liabilities			
Creditors		60,000	
Working Capital			101,650
Net Assets			121,400
Financed by:			
Share Capital	100,000		
Net Profit	1,400		
		101,400	
Bank Loan		20,000	
			121,400
			121,400

2 Accounting ratio calculations

(a) margins

$$\frac{5,000}{65,000} \times 100 = \textbf{7.69\%}$$

(b) mark-up

$$\frac{5,000}{60,000} \times 100 = \textbf{8.33\%}$$

or:

$$\frac{7.69}{92.31} \times 100 = \textbf{8.33\%}$$

(c) net profit margin

$$\frac{1,400}{65,000} \times 100 = \textbf{2.15\%}$$

(d) the return on capital employed attributable to the owner

average owner's capital employed:

$$\frac{100,000 + 101,400}{2} = 100,700$$

the return:

$$\frac{1,400}{100,700} \times 100 = \textbf{1.39\%}$$

(e) the return on capital employed (including loan)

average capital employed:

$$\frac{120,000 + 121,400}{2} = 120,700$$

the return:

$$\frac{1,750}{120,700} \times 100 = \textbf{1.45\%}$$

(f) working capital ratio

$$\frac{161{,}650}{60{,}000} = \textbf{2.69}$$

(g) quick ratio

$$\frac{116{,}650}{60{,}000} = \textbf{1.94}$$

(h) gearing (to owner's capital)

$$\frac{20{,}000}{101{,}400} = \textbf{0.20}$$

(i) gearing (to net assets)

$$\frac{20{,}000}{121{,}400} = \textbf{0.16}$$

(j) average stockturn

average stock:

$$\frac{45{,}000}{2} = 22{,}500$$

rate:

$$\frac{60{,}000}{22{,}500} = \textbf{2.67}$$

time stock is held on average:

$$\frac{45}{2.67} = \textbf{17 days}$$

(k) average debtor turnover

average debtors:

$$\frac{40{,}000}{2} = 20{,}000$$

rate:

$$\frac{40,000}{20,000} = 2$$

time taken to collect debts:

$$\frac{45}{2} = \textbf{23 days}$$

(I) average creditor turnover

average creditors:

$$\frac{60,000}{2} = 30,000$$

rate:

$$\frac{105,000}{30,000} = \textbf{3.50}$$

time taken to pay debts:

$$\frac{45}{3.5} = \textbf{13 days}$$

Notes

Since the business is new, I have taken the opening balances as 0 where required in the calculation to find the *average* balances. It might, in fact, be better to take them from the closing balances only and not divide by 2, in which case debtor, creditor and stock turnover rates would halve and number of days would double.

Although it is possible to calculate these ratios, they are very misleading in this instance. For example, it appears that we collect our debts, on average, every 23 days (or 46 if we ignore the opening balance of 0). In fact, we haven't yet collected anything. This illustrates, once more, that we should not take figures, ratios or anything else and use them without a clear understanding of how the figures are derived. In calculating debtor turnover, I have also deducted the *cash* sale from total sales.

In calculating the return on capital employed attributable to the owners, I have deducted the bank loan from the net assets when calculating the **average capital employed**.

In calculating the return on capital employed including the loan, I have added the loan interest to the net profit in calculating the **return**.

In both calculations for capital employed, I have included the money invested at the start of the period as the opening balances.

All these figures obviously relate to only a six week period; turnover rates would need to be multiplied by 8.67 (52 divided by 6) in order to find the equivalent annual figures (although these would be very misleading at this stage, as we have seen).

REASONS FOR BUSINESS FAILURES

Exercise H – Question

Your syndicate is to spend 20 minutes listing all the reasons a business might collapse. Write the list on the flip-chart, dividing items into categories as appropriate. Select a spokesperson to present and explain the list to the other syndicates afterwards.

REASONS FOR BUSINESS FAILURES

Exercise H – Answer

There are many potential causes of business failure and these may be categorised in various ways. In financial terms, lack of profitability is only the cause over a long period of time. Since profit is only an estimate of a business's surplus of income over expenses, subject to such assumptions as stock valuations, depreciation and so on, in itself it is a measure rather than an absolute. Many very profitable companies have gone bust throughout economic history simply because they are so profitable that they expand very rapidly without injecting sufficient additional working capital into the business – a term called over-trading. When this happens, the organisation may not have sufficient funds at any given time to pay a single creditor – all its profits are tied up in fixed assets with insufficient liquid resources to pay promptly. It is very sad when people lose their jobs and a successful business goes under simply because the people in charge concentrate on increasing profits rather than ensuring a positive cash flow. This comes as a nasty shock to the people who managed the business, who are often unaware of the dangers inherent in a rapidly expanding, successful organisation.

In order to combat the danger of negative cash flow, some companies even budget entirely on cashflow rather than profits. Profitability can be retrieved over a period of time, but not an illiquid situation – unless the creditors are very understanding and patient people.

One thing that must not be overlooked is that companies may be forced out of business or simply wound up by the owners out of choice (as opposed to necessity). For example, many modern split capital investment trust companies are established with a fixed life, with the obligation to cease trading and repay any surpluses to the owners on a given date according to the class of shares held. Many such companies provide the option for the owners on that date to vote in order to extend the life of the trust if they desire.

And so to just a few of the possible causes of business failures, starting with perhaps the most dangerous category, which is probably shortages of cash. This can be due to any of the following:

- too much of the profits taken out of the business by the owners
- too rapid expansion – too much extra stock purchased on credit
- too many assets are fixed rather than current
- poor cash flow planning

- failure of a major debtor
- extraordinary cash demands (e.g. legal action, sudden rent/rate increases, natural disasters and others, such as equipment breakdown,fire, accidents, changes in legislation requiring new equipment, staff and/or procedures)
- debtors allowed too long to pay
- sudden drop in sales
- strikes (internal and external)
- drastic currency fluctuations
- failure of organisation's bankers (remember BCCI?)
- large amounts of obsolete stock
- adverse verbal statements (remember Gerald Ratner?)
- fraud

There are many possible causes of the above (e.g. over-confidence, poor procedures for identifying and chasing unpaid debtors, failure to 'hedge' foreign sales and so on). The list at this level is almost endless. However, another set of causes may be identified which will have an effect over a longer period of time than the crises caused by the list above. These contribute to insufficient profitability in the medium- long-term:

- poor profit margins
- over-manning
- fierce competition (sometimes 'unfair')
- lack of competition
- long-term currency fluctuations
- new suppliers
- product life-cycles – reduced demand
- failure to change
- high overheads
- failure to re-invest in new equipment
- lack of research and development
- poor purchasing
- ineffective marketing
- changes in fashion
- changes in technology
- over-reliance on a few key customers

In the end, many of these causes must be laid at the door of poor management. There are other causes which can lead to the long-term demise of organisations and which can be specifically attributed to bad management
leading to poor:

- recruitment
- training
- motivation
- discipline
- objectives
- division of labour
- communication
- employee relations
- staff retention rates
- public relations and general reputation

When a business gets into trouble, it is the fault of the managers, not the accountants! This list, which has only scratched the surface, should indicate that financial analyses and awareness can identify many problems so that an early search for causes can be made in order to take decisive action – **in time**!

MISSING FIGURES

Exercise I – Question

We have selected information from four companies. Calculate the missing information for each company (round to the nearest pound, day and – in the case of margin, mark-up and rates – two decimal places.

	Company			
Information	**1**	**2**	**3**	**4**
Sales	150,000			
Gross Profit	25,000			
Cost of Sales		150,000		
% Margin			15	
% Mark-up		30		
Opening Stock	10,000		6,000	32,000
Purchases		125,000		
Closing Stock		20,000		30,000
Average Stock	15,000		8,000	
Stock Turnover Rate				
Days In Stock				
Opening Debtors	18,000		9,000	25,000
Closing Debtors		28,000		28,000
Average Debtors				
Debtor Turnover Rate		9		
Days To Receive Payment	50		35	45
Opening Creditors	10,000		9,000	21,000
Closing Creditors		12,500		17,000
Average Creditors		15,000	12,000	
Credit or Turnover Rate	6			4
Days To Pay			73	

MISSING FIGURES

Exercise I – Answer

Information	Company 1	2	3	4
Sales	150,000	195,000	65,884	214,915
Gross Profit	25,000	45,000	9,884	136,915
Cost Of Sales	125,000	150,000	56,000	78,000
% Margin	16.67	23.08	15	63.71
% Mark-up	20	30	17.65	175.56
Opening Stock	10,000	45,000	6,000	32,000
Purchases	135,000	125,000	60,000	76,000
Closing Stock	20,000	20,000	10,000	30,000
Average Stock	15,000	32,500	8,000	31,000
Stock Turnover Rate	8.33	4.62	7	2.52
Days In Stock	44	79	52	145
Opening Debtors	18,000	15,334	9,000	25,000
Closing Debtors	23,096	28,000	3,634	28,000
Average Debtors	20,548	21,667	6,317	26,500
Debtor Turnover Rate	7.3	9	10.43	8.11
Days To Receive Payment	50	41	35	45
Opening Creditors	10,000	17,500	9,000	21,000
Closing Creditors	35,000	12,500	15,000	17,000
Average Creditors	22,500	15,000	12,000	19,000
Creditor Turnover Rate	6	8.33	5	4
Days To Pay	61	44	73	91

CALCULATIONS

Company 1

Cost Of Sales: $150,000 - 25,000 = 125,000$

% Margin: $\dfrac{25,000}{150,000} \times 100 = 16.67$

% Mark-up: $\dfrac{25,000}{125,000} \times 100 = 20$ or $\dfrac{16.67}{83.33} \times 100 = 20$

Closing Stock: $(15,000 \times 2) - 10,000 = 20,000$

Purchases: $(10,000 + X) - 20,000 = 125,000$
therefore, $X = 135,000$

Stock Turnover Rate: $\dfrac{125,000}{15,000} = 8.33$

Days In Stock: $\dfrac{365}{8.33} = 44$

Debtor Turnover Rate: $\dfrac{365}{50} = 7.3$

Average Debtors: $\dfrac{150,000}{7.3} = 20,548$

Closing Debtors: $(20,548 \times 2) - 18,000 = 23,096$

Average Creditors: $\dfrac{135,000}{6} = 22,500$

Closing Creditors: $(22,500 \times 2) - 10,000 = 35,000$

Days To Pay: $\dfrac{365}{6} = 61$

Company 2

Gross Profit:

$$\frac{150,000}{100} \times 30 = 45,000$$

Sales:

$$150,000 + 45,000 = 195,000$$

% Margin:

$$\frac{45,000}{195,000} \times 100 = 23.08 \text{ or } \frac{30}{130} \times 100 = 23.08$$

Opening Stock:

$$X + 125,000 - 20,000 = 150,000$$
therefore, $X = 45,000$

Average Stock:

$$\frac{45,000 + 20,000}{2} = 32,500$$

Stock Turnover Rate:

$$\frac{150,000}{32,500} = 4.62$$

Days In Stock:

$$\frac{365}{4.62} = 79$$

Average Debtors:

$$\frac{195,000}{9} = 21,667$$

Opening Debtors:

$$(21,667 \times 2) - 28,000 = 15,334$$

Days To Receive Payment:

$$\frac{365}{9} = 41$$

Opening Creditors:

$$(15,000 \times 2) - 12,500 = 17,500$$

Creditor Turnover Rate:

$$\frac{125,000}{15,000} = 8.33$$

Days To Pay:

$$\frac{365}{8.33} = 44$$

Company 3

% Mark-up:	$\dfrac{15}{85} \times 100 = 17.65$

Closing Stock: $(8{,}000 \times 2) - 6{,}000 = 10{,}000$

Debtor Turnover Rate: $\dfrac{365}{35} = 10.43$

Closing Creditors: $(12{,}000 \times 2) - 9{,}000 = 15{,}000$

Creditor Turnover Rate: $\dfrac{365}{73} = 5$

Purchases: $5 \times 12{,}000 = 60{,}000$

Cost of Sales: $6{,}000 + 60{,}000 - 10{,}000 = 56{,}000$

Gross Profit: $\dfrac{56{,}000}{100} \times 17.65 = 9{,}884$

Sales: $56{,}000 + 9{,}884 = 65{,}884$

Stock Turnover Rate: $\dfrac{56{,}000}{8{,}000} = 7$

Days In Stock: $\dfrac{365}{7} = 52$

Average Debtors: $\dfrac{65{,}884}{10.43} = 6{,}317$

Closing Debtors: $(6{,}317 \times 2) - 9{,}000 = 3{,}634$

Company 4

Average Stock:

$$\frac{32,000 + 30,000}{2} = 31,000$$

Average Debtors:

$$\frac{25,000 + 28,000}{2} = 26,500$$

Debtor Turnover Rate:

$$\frac{365}{45} = 8.11$$

Sales:

$$26,500 \times 8.11 = 214,915$$

Average Creditors:

$$\frac{21,000 + 17,000}{2} = 19,000$$

Purchases:

$$4 \times 19,000 = 76,000$$

Cost of Sales:

$$32,000 + 76,000 - 30,000 = 78,000$$

Gross Profit:

$$214,915 - 78,000 = 136,915$$

% Margin:

$$\frac{136,915}{214,915} \times 100 = 63.71$$

% Mark-up:

$$\frac{63.71}{36.29} \times 100 = 175.56 \text{ or } \frac{136,915}{78,000} \times 100 = 175.53$$

Stock Turnover Rate:

$$\frac{78,000}{31,000} = 2.52$$

Days In Stock:

$$\frac{365}{2.52} = 145$$

Days To Pay:

$$\frac{365}{4} = 91$$

Session 6

....

Where do we go from here?

We have seen how to enter information in the accounts as transactions occur, summarise what has happened and establish the organisation's current position. In the last session, we learned how to assess the rewards which have been obtained, the efficiency with which they have been achieved and the risks which are involved.

Understanding what is happening now or in the past is very important if we are to be aware of our true performance and know what has been going on. After all, we cannot possibly be in control as managers if this is not the case. However, this does have one drawback; we cannot change the past. Usually, we are looking at financial information to plan future actions or control current ones. Looking at the past enables us to learn and assess where we have come from and the dangers and opportunities which may lie ahead. If we are not to be a rudderless boat, we must have and use this knowledge to plot a course for the future which will lead us to the land of opportunity while avoiding the rocks in between.

BUDGETARY CONTROL

Ask: what do you think is meant by the term, 'budgetary control'?
Answer: setting a budget and then making sure that you control what happens in practice against it. The budget is therefore a plan; like any plan, it needs to be closely monitored to make sure we are following it. Most successful military commanders pay close attention to planning; it is the same with successful organisations in civilian life.

Ask: what can we plan for in financial terms?
Answer: sales and expenses.

Ask: what about assets and liabilities?
Answer: yes!

Ask: what about return on capital employed?
Answer: yes!

125

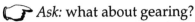 *Ask:* what about gearing?

Answer: yes! In fact, there is nothing which we have looked at – or will look at later – which cannot be part of your financial plan (in other words, the budget). If we have decided on our planned level of sales and expenses and are aware of how long it takes to collect and pay debts, we will know how much working capital we require. We will be able to establish what fixed assets will be needed and how much long-term capital must be used. We can draw up a projected Trading, Profit and Loss Account and Balance Sheet for the coming period and estimate all of the accompanying ratios which we looked at in the last session.

We can set a budget for any period we choose. The normal period is one year, although many organisations (especially capital-intensive manufacturers) also plan ahead over three to five year periods on a 'rolling' basis. The further ahead we plan, the more uncertainties will arise and the less accurate our plans will be. For some items (notably, cash flow) we will need to plan for much shorter periods. When we are making plans, we will need to look at the trends from previous periods, giving added weightings to those most recent. We will also have to consider anything which we know is likely to change in the future, such as new legislation, quotas, fashions or whatever else might affect the organisation and alter its current trajectory.

When we have taken note of what we know of at this point in time, we will consider the various options open to us for the future and determine what we would like to achieve. Objectives might be set on any number of areas – return on capital employed, sales, market share, cost control, diversification, expansion, increased liquidity and so on. Just about anything may be included. The only drawback, of course, is that we must determine *how* we are to achieve these objectives. Provided it is feasible to achieve the targets, we would next put the changes into practice in our projected Trading, Profit and Loss Account and Balance Sheet to see what the overall effects would be. A final decision must then be reached to determine if the overall effects of our plans are acceptable. The planning process requires a good deal of consultation right across the organisation. The quality and effectiveness of the plan ultimately depends on the accuracy and completeness of the information on which it is based, which is why you (and every manager) are intimately involved in the whole process.

In some organisations, budgeting commences at the sales level and works back to arrive at net profit; in others, net profit, then costs are calculated to end up at the required sales level. It is more important, however, to ensure that the budget as a whole is acceptable, realistic and desirable than to be over-concerned about which particular approach is adopted.

Let's go back to our working example Trading, Profit and Loss Account and Balance Sheet:

Trading, Profit and Loss Account for the Period 1.1 – 15.2

	%	£	£
Sales			69,000
Cost of Sales	85.51		59,000
Gross Profit	14.49		10,000
Operating Expenses			
Business Rates	0.72	500	
Salaries and Wages	1.45	1,000	
Printing and Stationery	7.97	5,500	
Telephone	0.67	4.60	
			7,460
Net Profit	3.68		2,540

Balance Sheet as at 15.2

	£	£
Fixed assets		
Premises	50,000	
Equipment	10,000	
		60,000
Current Assets		
Stock	21,000	
Debtors	32,000	
Bank	34,540	
	87,540	
Current Liabilities		
Creditors	45,000	
Working Capital		42,450
Net Assets		102,540
Financed by:		
Share Capital	100,000	
Undistributed Net Profit	2,450	
		102,540
		102,540

From our analysis in the previous session, we calculated the following:

Return on Capital Employed	2.51%
Current Ratio	1.95
Quick Ratio	1.48
Margin	14.49%
Mark-up	16.95%
Debtor Turnover Rate	3.37
Days Taken to Collect Money	13
Creditor Turnover Rate	3.56
Days Taken to Pay Money	13
Stock Turnover Rate	5.62
Days Stock is Held for	8

We must remember that this company started from scratch and that the period covered is only six weeks. The figures are therefore atypical of what would be expected in the future and over a longer period. The resulting ratios will be highly distorted given that stock, debtors and creditors were '0' at the period start, so that our average figures (in future) are more likely to be closer to the closing balances of the first period. If we took (in this instance) the closing balances to be the averages (instead of dividing them by 2 as we did originally to get an average), then the turnover rates would halve and the number of days would double.

For the purpose of simplicity, we will pretend that the business is not new, and that our ratios *are* derived from normal, ongoing figures. On this basis, we can set about establishing a budget for the *next* six weeks.

We will start by setting some targets for the forthcoming periods. We can choose whatever we like – provided it is achievable, desirable and acceptable. Let's suppose that we create the following plan:

Target	Method
increase net profit to £4,000	increase sales by spending £2,000 on local advertising; reduce prices to boost sales by reducing margins to 11%; allow customers longer to pay – 15 days on average
take account of reduced asset values	depreciate equipment by 6%
make more efficient use of working capital	increase stockturn rate to 6 by implementing a new ordering system; extend payment period to creditors to 18 days
pay a dividend of £3,000	pay from the net profit earned during the period

We have sufficient information to see how things would be affected. We would make the following changes:

1 Amend the net profit figure to £4,000.
2 Insert under operating expenses Advertising (£2,000) and Depreciation (6% of £10,000, which is £600).
3 Calculate the new gross profit by adding the new totals for net profit and operating expenses. Operating expenses come to £10,060; gross profit will therefore be £14,060.
4 Change the margin to 11 per cent and calculate sales (14,060 divided by 11, then multiplied by 100). This comes to £127,818.
5 Calculate the cost of sales and then amend the remaining figures (which will have changed) in the percentage column.
6 Enter the dividend and calculate the outstanding balance on the account.

Let's look at the projected Trading, Profit and Loss Account first (show OHP):

Budgeted Trading, Profit and Loss Account for the Period 16.2 – 31.3

	%	£	£
Sales			127,818
Cost of Sales	89.00		113.758
Gross Profit	11.00		14,060
Operating Expenses			
Business Rates	0.39	500	
Salaries and Wages	0.78	1,000	
Printing and Stationery	4.30	5,500	
Advertising	1.56	2,000	
Telephone	0.36	460	
Depreciation	0.47	600	
			10,060
Net Profit	3.13		4,000
Dividend			3,000
			1,000
Undistributed Profit b/f			2,540
Undistributed Profit c/f			3,540

We could easily have altered other operating expenses as and where applicable. In the example, we can assume that the business was operating with excess capacity and can therefore increase sales without increasing existing overheads. As a result (and because sales have increased), the percentages of existing operating expenses to the new sales figure have decreased. It is interesting that the net profit margin has also gone down – despite an increase in actual net profit.

Now let's consider how our Balance Sheet will change:

1 Alter the 'financed by' section to show how this will be affected by the Net Profit for the period, the dividend paid and the *new* undistributed profit figure.

2 Amend the fixed assets to incorporate depreciation.

3 Calculate the closing stock by dividing cost of sales by 6 to give *average* stock; double this figure and deduct opening stock (the figure in the Balance Sheet at the close of the preceding period).

4 Calculate the new closing debtors figure; divide the days taken to collect money (15) into 44; divide sales by this figure (which is the new *debtor turnover rate*) to give *average debtors*; multiply by 2 and subtract opening debtors.

5 Calculate the new closing creditors figure; calculate *purchases* by adding the closing stock to cost of sales and then deducting the opening stock (from the balance sheet at the end of the previous period); calculate the *creditor turnover rate* by dividing 44 by 18; divide this into purchases to give *average creditors*; multiply this figure by 2 and deduct opening creditors.

6 From the new net assets figure (which must equal the new 'financed by total'), we can deduct the new fixed assets balance to give us the new working capital. If we add the new creditors figure (in this case, the only current liability) we arrive at current assets; this allows us to calculate the only remaining figure which has not been altered – the new bank balance.

We can now look at our projected Balance Sheet:

Budgeted Balance Sheet as at 31.3

	£	£	£
Fixed Assets			
Premises		50,000	
Equipment	10,000		
Depreciation	600		
		9,400	
			59,400
Current Assets			
Stock		16,920	
Debtors		55,148	
Bank		16,808	
		88,876	
Current Liabilities			
Creditors		44,736	
Working Capital			44,140
Net Assets			103,540
Financed by:			
Share Capital		100,000	
Net Profit For Period	4,000		
Dividend	3,000		
	1,000		
Undistributed Net Profit b/f	2,540		
Undistributed Net Profit		3,540	
			103,540
			103,540

Pause and ensure people follow all that you have done and agree the calculations.

Ask: now that we have our budgeted Trading, Profit and Loss Account and Balance Sheet for the next period, what else can we do?
Answer: we can analyse the performance and situation which we can expect at the end of the next period.

Get everyone to make the calculations, then go through each ratio and agree their answers, which should be as follows:

	1.1 – 15.2	Budget For 16.2 – 31.3
Return on Capital Employed:	2.51%	3.44%
Current Ratio:	1.95	1.99
Quick Ratio:	1.48	1.61
Margin:	14.49%	11%
Mark-up:	16.95%	12.36%
Debtor Turnover Rate:	3.37	2.93
Days Taken to Collect Money:	13	15
Creditor Turnover Rate:	3.56	2.44
Days Taken To Pay Money:	13	18
Stock Turnover Rate:	5.62	6
Days Stock is Held for:	8	7

Share evaluation

At this stage, it is interesting to look at another aspect of performance. Share capital is £100,000; let's assume that this is made up of 100,000 shares which were issued at £1 each. On a net assets valuation basis on 31.3 they would be worth £1.0354 each. However, stock market valuations rarely fall in line with a net assets valuation basis. Because the business is producing a very healthy rate of return (3.44% in six weeks), the shares are in great demand and are trading at a mid-market price of £1.20. This represents a premium to the net asset value of the shares of 15.9 per cent. In the budgeted period, a dividend of £3,000 was paid – in effect, three pence per share. If the figures related to a full year (rather than merely six weeks), we can calculate that the **yield** is:

$$\frac{\text{dividend}}{\text{price of share}} \times 100 = \frac{0.03}{1.20} \times 100 = 2.5\%$$

The yield represents the percentage income an investor will receive on their investment, subject to the share price and dividend staying the same in the future, which is extremely unlikely!

We can also consider the **earnings per share (EPS)**. This represents the total return to the investor, because it is based on the net profit rather than the dividend. If we assume that the share price will increase by future undistributed profit (net assets will), it is reasonable to reflect this capital growth in our total return as well as dividend income. We would calculate earnings per share thus:

$$\frac{\text{Net Profit}}{\text{Number of Shares}} = \frac{4,000}{100,000} = 0.04$$

In other words, four pence per share.

Finally, we will consider the number of years it would take to recoup our investment, although once more this is a very rough estimate as share prices and future profits are constantly changing:

$$\frac{\text{price of share}}{\text{earnings per share}} = \frac{1.20}{0.04} = 30$$

Once more, we have assumed our figures relate to one year and so our **price/ earnings**, or **P/E** ratio represents 30 years – quite a high figure in the UK but not unknown. The yield and P/E ratio are shown for most listed companies in the *Financial Times*, along with the current mid-market share price and the high and low points it has reached within the last year.

Accepting and controlling the budget

Now we will turn back to our budgeted figures and consider them in comparison with the historical performance from the previous period. We can either accept our budget or reject it and try again.

Ask: would you recommend accepting the budget?
Answer: yes. As we have mentioned, the return on capital employed is very healthy and represents a 37per cent increase on the previous period. Our liquidity position (on both measures) has improved, with stocks and creditors being reduced and working capital increased. This leaves us with sufficient money in the bank to allow for expansion as the business grows. Our debtor, creditor and stock turnover rates are in line with our targets, naturally – and

all this on a reduced gross profit margin (and, for that matter, net profit margin). It would therefore appear that the budget would be accepted, provided that the increased sales are attainable and existing operating expenses can be controlled.

Having set our objectives, drawn up our budget and accepted it, we have to do one more thing at this stage.

☞ *Ask:* what do we need to do next?

Answer: draw up some control documents to check (as we go along) that we are meeting our objectives in practice. Some organisations use percentages to compare the actual figures with the planned ones, since percentages are more useful than absolute figures in this instance. They sometimes go on from there and 'home' in on **variances** of more than a set percentage. This is particularly used in **cost accounting**, which is designed to control costs in the manufacturing process at the level of each individual unit which is produced. It may also be referred to as part of a process called **management by exception**.

Control documents, like budgets themselves, can be as simple or as complicated as necessary. They are based on **control periods**; the shorter the period, the more quickly variances can be spotted and problems or opportunities attended to. With finances, the sooner we become aware of something, the more options and therefore control we will have. Again, it is like steering a boat – the sooner we spot the rocks, the more chance we will have to avoid them; if we see a better course than anticipated in time, we can take advantage of it. Let's look at a very simple control document (see opposite).

Because we are dealing with expenses in this control document, a negative variance is good in that it indicates that we have spent less than we budgeted for. The reverse would be true if this were a sales control document. Be very careful about positive and negative variances; some organisations portray them the opposite way round, i.e. an overspend on budget is shown as a negative purely because negative is viewed as bad.

☞ *Ask:* what is the first thing you should do when presented with a table of figures?

Answer: make absolutely sure that you understand where the figures come from and how they are worked out.

In our example operating expense control document, you will notice that the overall variances tend to get smaller as time goes on. This is because one week in isolation can distort things quite considerably but the averages over a slightly longer period will even things out to give a better picture. Note also

Budgeted control document for expenses for six weeks to 31.3

Week 1

Operating expense	Budget	Actual	% Variance	Running totals Budget	Actual	% Variance
Business Rates	–	–	–	–	–	–
Salaries and Wages	167	200	19.76	167	200	19.76
Printing and Stationery	1,500	1,300	(13.33)	1,500	1,300	(13.33)
Advertising	1,000	850	(15.00)	1,000	850	(15.00)
Telephone	–	–	–	–	–	–
Depreciation	100	100	0	100	100	0
Total	2,767	2,450	(11.46)	2,767	2,450	(11.46)

Week 1

Operating expense	Budget	Actual	% Variance	Running totals Budget	Actual	% Variance
Business Rates	250	250	0	250	250	0
Salaries and Wages	167	150	(10.18)	334	350	4.79
Printing and Stationery	250	300	20.00	1,750	1,600	(8.57)
Advertising	300	400	33.33	1,300	1,250	(3.85)
Telephone	230	275	19.57	230	275	19.57
Depreciation	100	100	0	200	200	0
Total	1,297	1,475	13.72	4,064	3,925	(3.42)

that when drawing up the budget for each control period you cannot simply divide the total budget figures for the period by the number of weeks covered, since expenses will vary from week to week. For example, you may pay the telephone bill only once every month. The same principle would apply to the control document for sales, where a company is certain to sell more products at certain times of the year than others; for example, a department store would probably expect a huge proportion of its sales for the year to be made in the last few weeks leading up to Christmas.

Each control document could be far more detailed if this is practical and useful. For instance, the one for sales could be broken down into the sales for each product, and/or for each sales person or branch. Another control document may be drawn up to calculate the net profit figures, provided an accurate assessment of the actual gross profit earned can be made without a stock-take (remember, cost of sales is calculated using the opening and closing stock as well as purchases and includes any stock lost or destroyed).

There is one budget which is most important and the control document is vital.

☞ *Ask:* what is it?

Answer: cash! We have already seen that cash is, in fact, more important than profit, especially in the short-term. When we budget for cash flow, we are not interested in profit or loss, so to that extent it is quite different from the other elements of budgeting. If an organisation only draws up one budget, it should be for cash. Any business which does not draw up a cash budget is dicing with corporate death.

In simple terms, a cash budget will be concerned with every inflow and outflow of actual money, whatever the source and for whatever purpose. We would therefore be concerned with expenses which are *paid*, the payment of debts to and from the organisation and payments for any other reason (such as purchase of fixed assets, dividend payments and so on). Depreciation would therefore not enter into the cash budget.

☞ *Ask:* why not?

Answer: because it does not involve a movement of cash; it is an accounting entry to reflect the devaluation of an asset.

For any overall period, the cash budget calculation would be similar to that for stock. We would know our opening balance, add the inflows of cash from whatever source and deduct the outflows of cash for whatever purpose. This would enable us to estimate our anticipated closing balance. However, this is not suffi-

Cash budget control document for six weeks to 31.3

✎ Week 1

Inflows	Budget	Actual	Variance
Opening Balance	34,540	34,540	
Cash Sales	–	–	
Payments from Debtors	17,230	15,130	(2,100)
Bank Interest	–	–	
Sales of Fixed Assets	–	–	
VAT Refunds	–	–	
Other Receipts	–	–	
Total	51,770	49,670	(2,100)

Outflows	Budget	Actual	Variance
Business Rates	–	–	
Salaries and Wages	167	200	33
Printing and Stationery	500	450	(50)
Advertising	500	425	(75)
Telephone	–	–	
Dividends	–	–	
Payments to Creditors	24,231	25,200	969
Purchase of Fixed Assets	–	–	
Bank Charges	–	–	
VAT Payments	–	–	
Corporation Tax Payments	–	–	
Other Payments	–	–	
Total	25,398	26,275	877
Closing Balance	26,372	23,395	(2,977)

✎ **Week 2**

Inflows	Budget	Actual	Variance	To date
Opening Balance	26,372	23,395	(2,977)	(877)
Cash Sales	–	–		
Payments from Debtors	14,770	16,870	2,100	
Bank Interest	–	–		
Sales of Fixed Assets	–	–		
VAT Refunds	–	–		
Other Receipts	–	–		
Total	41,142	40,265		
Outflows				
Business Rates	250	250		
Salaries and Wages	167	170	3	
Printing and Stationery	1,000	850	(150)	
Advertising	350	375	25	
Telephone	230	245	15	
Dividends	–	–		
Payments to Creditors	20,769	20,500	(269)	
Purchase of Fixed Assets	–	–		
Bank Charges	–	–		
VAT Payments	–	–		
Corporation Tax Payments	–	–		
Other Payments	–	–		
Total	22,766	22,390		(376)
Closing Balance	18,376	17,875		(501)

cient because we need to know most accurately when we can expect the inflows and outflows to occur and what our cash position will be at any time – especially where we have very low levels of working capital and a low quick ratio.

Let's consider a simple cash budget control document for our example business for the first two weeks (see overleaf).

Note: go through the layout and calculations and ensure everyone fully understands how the cash budget for each week is drawn up.

This time, the variance columns show absolute figures rather than percentages. When we are dealing with cash, the amount is quite important – but there is no reason why we can't show both absolute figures and percentages. As you can see, though, even with very limited information for two short control periods, we need a lot of space to lay the information out clearly. That is why budget control documentation is so detailed and bulky in real life. It's not that it's very complicated; it just needs to provide a lot of simple (but important) information. Since individuals only need to worry about the parts which concern them, there is no cause to be put off just because there are many pages of data.

Note: at this point, it might be useful to examine the actual budget documentation which the trainees use. Often, such documentation is quite straightforward and having arrived at this point in the training it should be a lot more meaningful to them.

The cash budget, as we have said, is particularly important, and is especially vital in the short term (when we will have less time to correct a negative cash-flow position). It is also important in the medium to long term.

☞ *Ask:* why?
Answer: if our liquid resources are inadequate, we may need to arrange for increased long-term funding. This could be achieved by issuing more shares, debentures (fixed interest loan stock), or arranging a bank loan.
☞ *Ask:* suppose our liquid resources are higher than necessary?
Answer: we may be able to use some of them more effectively elsewhere. Remember that, generally, less liquid investments offer a higher return.

Cash flow

Good! There is just one other document which you may come across. It is included with the Trading, Profit and Loss Account and Balance Sheet of an organisation above a certain size when it produces a full annual report (as opposed to abbreviated accounts). This document is called the Cash Flow

Statement. Its purpose is to illustrate the changes in cash during the period, from all sources (which is why I have decided to cover it here). There are two methods for drawing up a Cash Flow Statement. We shall look at these in relation to our working example, starting with the **Gross Method** (also known as the **Direct Method**.

Budgeted Cash Flow Statement for Period 15.2 – 31.3

Operating Activities		
Cash Received from Customers	104,670	
Cash Paid to Suppliers	(109,942)	
Cash Paid to Employees	(1,000)	
Other Cash Payments	(8,460)	
Net Cash Inflow from Operating Activities		(14,732)
Returns On Investements And Servicing Of Finance		
Interest Received	–	
Interest Paid	–	
Dividends Paid	(3,000)	
Net Cash Inflow from Returns on Investments and Servicing of Finance		(3,000)
Tax Paid		–
Investing Activities		
Payments for Acquisition of Fixed Assets	–	
Receipts from Sale of Fixed Assets	–	
Net Outflow from Investing Activities		–
Net Cash Inflow before Financing		(17,732)
Financing		
Issue of Ordinary Share Capital	–	
Net Cash Inflow from Financing		–
Increase in Cash and Cash Equivalents		(17,732)

The decrease of £17,732 will be reflected in the change in cash held over the period covered. This change will be the difference between the bank balances in the Balance Sheets at the start and end of the period. As with the Trading, Profit and Loss Account and Balance Sheet, some of the figures detailed are sometimes shown as notes to the Cash Flow Statement rather than in the document itself.

To calculate the cash received from customers, I have taken the opening debtors (since they will all have paid in the period covered by the Cash Flow Statement), added sales and deducted the closing debtors figure (so that sales for which cash has been received during the period are included).

To calculate cash paid to suppliers, I have taken opening creditors (who will all have been paid in the period), added purchases (which I calculated earlier) and subtracted closing creditors.

Other cash payments would be all the operating expenses paid during the period apart from salaries and wages (shown as a separate item) and depreciation.

☞ *Ask:* why have I excluded depreciation?
Answer: because it is not an expense which involves an actual outflow of funds. Although we deducted it to arrive at our net profit, the funds never left the business (unlike all our other expenses) so we must not show them as an outflow of cash here.

The alternative method for drawing up a Cash Flow Statement is known as the **Net** (or **Indirect**) Method. The difference is in the operating activities section, which would look like this:

Budgeted Cash Flow Statement for Period 15.2 – 31.3

Operating Activities		
Operating Profit	4,000	
Depreciation	600	
Decrease in Stock	4,080	
Increase in Debtors	(23,148)	
Decrease in Creditors	(264)	
Net Cash Inflow from Operating Activities		(14,732)

Using this method, our starting point is operating profit. Depreciation must be added back (since, as we know, it did not involve an outflow of cash yet was deducted in the Trading, Profit and Loss Account when calculating operating profit). We now take account of changes in working capital to see how the cash element will have changed during the period.

Stocks have decreased, releasing more cash into the business. Debtors have increased, using up more cash; the increase is therefore shown as a negative figure. The decrease in creditors means that they are providing less funds for use in the business thus also creating a reduction in cash; it is therefore also shown as a negative figure.

I will now summarise the main points from this session:

- a budget is a financial plan

- every aspect of finance can be budgeted for

- **budgeting** involves setting targets

- **control** involves monitoring progress against those targets

- everyone should be involved in creating budgets and in monitoring progress

- share prices may trade at a *premium* or *discount* to their net asset value

- the **yield** represents the historical percentage income received based on the current share price

- **earnings per share** or **EPS**, is the latest annual total return per share, including both income and net asset value appreciation

- the **price-earning** or **P/E** ratio tells us how many years it would take to recoup the current share price based on the latest annual earnings per share

- control documents allow us to monitor progress against budgets

- percentage **variances** are often used to highlight major differences between budgeted and actual figures

- positive and negative figures may be used in different ways to illustrate variances

- budget documentation may be bulky and look complicated but is usually straightforward

- the **cash** budget is **most** important

- a Cash Flow Statement illustrates the changes in **cash** between two Balance Sheet dates.

Note: for the next two exercises, trainees will also need to refer to the answers to Exercise F; leave it up to them to realise this, unless they really get stuck.

BUDGETED TRADING, PROFIT AND LOSS ACCOUNT; BALANCE SHEET AND CASH FLOW STATEMENT

Exercise J – Question

The company in Exercise D has set the following objectives for the coming year:

1 Create a positive working capital position by reducing the overdraft to £10,000.

2 Pay the maximum possible dividend out of the net profit for the year after allowing for the effects of the previous objective.

3 Increase sales by 10 per cent. This will necessitate an increase in advertising of £5,000; other operating expenses (except depreciation) will increase by 5 per cent.

4 Write down the value of the fixed assets by the same amount as was charged in the previous period.

Draw up the budgeted Trading, Profit and Loss Account, Balance Sheet and Cash Flow Statement as at the end of the forthcoming period. For the Cash Flow Statement, use the Gross Method but show the difference that would occur in the operating activities section if the Net Method is used.

BUDGETED TRADING, PROFIT AND LOSS ACCOUNT; BALANCE SHEET AND CASH FLOW STATEMENT

Exercise J – Answer

Budgeted Trading, Profit and Loss Account for the Year Ending 31.12

	%	£	£
Sales			228,030
Cost of Sales	53.45		121,882
Gross Profit	46.55		106,148
Operating Expenses			
Business Rates	2.49	5,670	
Salaries and Wages	11.51	26,250	
Advertising and Display	8.11	18,500	
Administration	2.49	5,670	
Depreciation	7.46	17,000	
			73,090
Net Profit	14.50		33,058
Dividend			19,917
Undistributed Net Profit			13,141

Budgeted Balance Sheet as at 31.12

	£	£	£
Fixed Assets			
Premises		75,000	
Motor Vehicles	48,000		
Depreciation	24,000		
		24,000	
Fixtures and Fittings	20,000		
Depreciation	10,000		
		10,000	
			109,000
Current Assets			
Stock		18,730	
Debtors		22,089	
		40,819	
Current Liabilities			
Creditors	6,478		
Bank	10,000		
		16,478	
Working Capital			24,341
Net Assets			133,341
Financed by:			
Share Capital		90,000	
Undistributed Net Profit B/F	30,200		
Net Profit for Year	33,058		
	63,258		
Dividend	19,917		
		43,341	
			133,341
			133,341

Budgeted Cash Flow Statement for Period 1.1 – 31.12

Operating Activities

Cash Received from Customers	223,441	
Cash Paid to Suppliers	(141,934)	
Cash Paid to Employees	(26,250)	
Other Cash Payments	(29,840)	
Net Cash Inflow from Operating Activities		25,417

Returns On Investments and Servicing of Finance

Interest Received	–	
Interest Paid	–	
Dividends Paid	(19,917)	
Net Cash Inflow from Returns on Investments and Servicing of Finance		(19,917)

Tax Paid   –

Investing Activities

Payments for Acquisition of Fixed Assets	–	
Receipts from Sale of Fixed Assets	–	
Net Outflow from Investing Activities		–
Net Cash Inflow before Financing		(5,500)

Financing

Issue of Ordinary Share Capital	–	
Net Cash Inflow from Financing		–
Increase in Cash and Cash Equivalents		(5,500)

If using the Net Method, the first section of the Cash Flow Statement would look like this:

Operating Activities

Operating Profit	33,058	
Depreciation	17,000	
Increase in Stock	(2,030)	
Increase in Debtors	(4,589)	
Decrease in Creditors	(18,022)	
Net Cash Inflow from Operating Activities		(25,417)

Notes

1 Assuming the gross profit margin remains the same, we can calculate the cost of sales and the gross profit.

2 Assuming the turnover rates remain the same, we can calculate closing stock by dividing cost of sales by the stock turnover rate (6.88) to give *average stock*; we then double this figure and deduct the opening stock (16,700) to leave closing stock.

3 Now that we know opening stock, closing stock and cost of sales, we can calculate purchases.

4 If we divide purchases by the creditor turnover rate (8), we arrive at *average creditors*; multiply this by 2 and deduct opening creditors and we arrive at closing creditors.

5 We can divide sales by the debtor turnover rate (11.52) to calculate *average debtors*; double this and deduct opening debtors to arrive at closing debtors.

6 The only missing figure in the Balance Sheet is the dividend, which we can now calculate.

7 Cash received from customers is £17,500 (opening debtors) plus £228,030 (sales), minus £22,089 (closing debtors).

8 Cash paid to suppliers is £24,500 (opening creditors) plus £123,912 (purchases, calculated when establishing closing creditors – notes 3 and 4 above), minus £6,478 (closing creditors).

9 Other payments are total operating expenses, less salaries and wages and depreciation.

BUDGETED TRADING, PROFIT AND LOSS ACCOUNT; BALANCE SHEET AND CASH FLOW STATEMENT

Exercise K – Question

The company in Exercise E has set the following objectives for the coming year:

1 Increase sales to £500,000 by reducing the gross profit margin to 50 per cent.

2 Increase stock turnover to a rate of 5 by introducing a new computerised stock control system. This will increase the general expenses to £10,200.

3 Other operating expenses will increase by 10 per cent.

4 New premises costing £48,000 are to be purchased; these are to be depreciated by 25 per cent.

5 Depreciation on existing assets will be the same as in the previous year.

6 Drawings of £50,000 are to be paid.

Draw up the budgeted Trading, Profit and Loss Account, Balance Sheet and Cash Flow Statement as at the end of the forthcoming period. For the Cash-Flow Statement, use the Indirect Method but show the difference in the operating activities section if the Direct Method is used.

BUDGETED TRADING, PROFIT AND LOSS ACCOUNT; BALANCE SHEET AND CASH FLOW STATEMENT

Exercise K – Answer

Budgeted Trading, Profit and Loss Account for the Year Ending 5.4

	%	£	£
Sales			500,000
Cost of Sales	50.00		250,000
Gross Profit	50.00		250,000
Operating Expenses			
Business Rates	1.87	9,350	
Salaries and Wages	12.10	60,500	
Advertising and Display	2.71	13,530	
General Expenses	2.04	10,200	
Depreciation	11.80	59,000	
			152,580
Net Profit	19.48		97,420
Drawings			50,000
Undistributed Net Profit			47,420

Bugeted Balance Sheet as at 5.4

	£	£	£
Fixed Assets			
Premises	148,000		
Depreciation	62,000		
		86,000	
Motor Vehicles	60,000		
Depreciation	30,000		
		30,000	
Fixtures and Fittings	16,000		
Depreciation	8,000		
		8,000	
Equipment	12,000		
Depreciation	6,000		
		6,000	
			130,000
Current Assets			
Stock		65,800	
Debtors		63,954	
Bank		28,334	
		158,088	
Current Liabilities			
Creditors		40,568	
Working Capital			117,520
Net Assets			247,520
Financed by:			
Capital		150,000	
Undistributed Net Profit B/F	50,100		
Net Profit for Year	97,420		
	147,520		
Drawings	50,000		
		97,520	
			247,520
			247,520

Budgeted Cash Flow Statement for Period 6.4–5.4

Operating Activities

Operating Profit	97,420	
Depreciation	59,000	
Increase in Stock	(31,600)	
Increase in Debtors	(30,254)	
Increase in Creditors	16,068	
Net Cash Inflow from Operating Activities		110,634

Returns on Investments and Servicing of Finance

Interest Received	–	
Interest Paid	–	
Drawings Paid	(50,000)	
Net Cash Inflow from Returns on Investments and Servicing of Finance		(50,000)

Tax Paid		–

Investing Activities

Payments for Acquisition of Fixed Assets	(48,000)	
Receipts from Sale of Fixed Assets	–	
Net Outflow from Investing Activities		(48,000)
Net Cash Inflow before Financing		12,634

Financing

Issue of Ordinary Share Capital	–	
Net Cash Inflow from Financing		–
Increase in Cash and Cash Equivalents		(12,634)

If using the Direct Method, the first section of the Cash Flow Statement would look like this:

Operating Activities

Cash Received from Customers	468,246	
Cash Paid to Suppliers	(263,532)	
Cash Paid to Employees	(60,500)	
Other Cash Payments	(33,580)	
Net Cash Inflow from Operating Activities		110,634

Notes

1 We can use the new gross profit margin to calculate the cost of sales and the gross profit, based on our new sales figure.

2 We can calculate closing stock by dividing cost of sales by the new stock turnover rate (5) to give *average stock*; we then double this figure and deduct the opening stock (34,200) to leave closing stock.

3 Now that we know opening stock, closing stock and cost of sales, we can calculate purchases.

4 If we divide purchases by the creditor turnover rate (8.93), we arrive at *average creditors*; multiply this by 2 and deduct opening creditors and we arrive at closing creditors.

5 We can divide sales by the debtor turnover rate (10.4) to calculate *average debtors*; double this and deduct opening debtors to arrive at closing debtors.

6 The only missing figure in the Balance Sheet is the bank, which we can now calculate.

7 Cash received from customers is £32,200 (opening debtors) plus £500,000 (sales), minus £63,954 (closing debtors).

8 Cash paid to suppliers is £22,500 (opening creditors) plus £281,600 (purchases, calculated when establishing closing creditors – notes 3 and 4 above), minus £40,568 (closing creditors).

9 Other payments are total operating expenses, less salaries and wages and depreciation.

10 Pre-paid insurance at the start of the period has been deducted from the increase in debtors in the Indirect Method format; advertising owed at the start has been deducted from the increase in creditors in the same section. In the Direct Method format, the difference between these two items (£500 owed *by* the company) has been added to the other cash payments.

CASH BUDGETING

Exercise L – Question

From the following information, draw up a simple budget in any format you choose to highlight the company's cash position at the end of each month from October to March (inclusive).

Balance Sheet as at 30.9

	£	£	£
Fixed Assets			
Premises	250,000		
Depreciation	50,000		
		200,000	
Motor Vehicles	100,000		
Depreciation	25,000		
		75,000	
Plant and Machinery	60,000		
Depreciation	30,000		
		30,000	
			305,000
Current Assets			
Stock		58,730	
Debtors		34,600	
Bank		45,500	
		138,330	
Current Liabilities			
Creditors		44,300	
Working Capital			94,030
Net Assets			399,030
Financed by:			
Share Capital		200,000	
Undistributed Net Profit b/f	169,030		
Net Profit for Year	105,000		
	274,030		
Dividend	75,000		
		199,030	
			399,030
			399,030

Notes

1 The following additional information is available:

Month	Sales	Operating Costs
October	75,000	8,000
November	78,000	10,000
December	135,000	15,000
January	100,000	11,000
February	65,000	7,000
March	55,000	8,000

2 An interim dividend of £35,000 will be paid on 28.2.

3 Terms for debtors are one month.

4 Six weeks credit is obtained from suppliers.

5 Assume that sales and purchases for any given month are spread equally throughout that month.

6 A 25 per cent mark-up is applied to all stock sold.

7 Assume that purchases are made during the same month as they are sold and that underlying stock levels remain constant.

8 Assume that existing creditors arose from purchases which were spread evenly in value throughout the preceding six weeks.

CASH BUDGETING

Exercise L – Answer

Cash Budget

October

Opening bal. b/f	45,500
Payments to creditors:	
$\frac{4}{6} \times 44,300 =$	(29,533)
	15,967
Operating costs	(8,000)
	7,967
Receipts from debtors	34,600
Bal. 31.10	42,567

November

Payments to creditors:		
$\frac{2}{6} \times 44,300$	14,767	
$\frac{1}{2} \times 60,000$	30,000	
		(44,767)
		(2,200)
Operating costs		(10,000)
		(12,200)
Receipts from debtors		75,000
Bal. 30.11		62,800

December

Payments to creditors:

$\frac{1}{2} \times 60,000$	30,000	
$\frac{1}{2} \times 62,400$	31,200	
		(61,200)
		1,600
Operating costs		(15,000)
		(13,400)
Receipts from debtors		78,000
Bal. 31.12		64,600

January

Payments to creditors:

$\frac{1}{2} \times 62,400$	31,200	
$\frac{1}{2} \times 108,000$	54,000	
		(85,200)
		(20,600)
Operating costs		(11,000)
		(31,600)
Receipts from debtors		135,000
Bal. 31.1		103,400

February

Payments to creditors:

$\frac{1}{2} \times 108{,}000$ 54,000

$\frac{1}{2} \times 80{,}000$ 40,000

	(94,000)
	9,400
Operating costs	(7,000)
	2,400
Receipts from debtors	100,000
	102,400
Dividend	(35,000)
Bal. 28.2	67,400

March

Payments to creditors:

$\frac{1}{2} \times 80{,}000$ 40,000

$\frac{1}{2} \times 52{,}000$ 26,000

	(66,000)
	1,400
Operating costs	(8,000)
	(6,600)
Receipts from debtors	65,000
Bal. 31.3	58,400

Notes

1 We can calculate the creditors arising each month by calculating the cost of sales, which will be 80 per cent of sales because if the mark-up is 25 per cent, the margin must be 20 per cent. Since underlying stock levels are to remain unchanged and stock is purchased in the same month in which it is to be sold, purchases will, in effect, equal cost of sales.

2 Debtors arising in one month will be the same as sales for that month. Since credit is allowed for one month, debtors paying will be the same as the previous month's sales figure (or opening debtors in the case of October).

3 Creditors are paid every six weeks, so half of those arising in the previous month will be paid in the current month. Payment will also be made in the current month to outstanding creditors in the month before last. Since creditors at the start arose at even value in the six weeks prior to the budget period, four- sixths of the money would be paid in the first month (October).

4 This budget layout has taken the worst case scenario each month, in that it has deducted all the outgoings before adding the receipts. In practice, we would expect the receipts to arrive before all the outgoings occur.

Session 7

....

So what *is* the bottom line?

We have seen that cash is much more important than profit in the short and even medium term. However, it is inescapable that, in the long term, even though cash is still vital it is net profit which is the main objective of a commercial organisation. Even non-commercial organisations will need to ensure that, over time, their income exceeds their expenses. In the short and medium terms, cash may ensure survival but without a surplus the organisation will slowly bleed to death. Provided that we have ensured a positive cash flow to guarantee our survival for a reasonable period, we must now therefore turn our attention to net profit.

In order to survive some way into the future, we may be able to exist without a surplus provided that we can at least break even. The break-even point is reached when the organisation's income exactly matches its expenses. If we reach this point we at least know that we are not making a loss. There is a way in which we can determine the level of sales which are required in order to reach the break-even point. The method also allows us to calculate how much net profit we will earn at any higher level of sales.

Ask: does that sound interesting?

Answer: yes! Such a tool could be of great assistance in decision making; even a non-profit making organisation will be able to plan the level of income required in order to meet its expenses. A manager in a commercial organisation would be able to use the technique to help determine the best project to allocate resources to in terms of its profitability and risk level. I am now going to explain the technique to you; we will start by taking yet another look at the Trading, Profit and Loss Account for our working example (show OHP).

Trading, Profit and Loss Account for the Period 1.1 - 15.2

	%	£	£
Sales			69,000
Cost of Sales	85.51		59,000
Gross Profit	14.49		10,000
Operating Expenses			
Business Rates	0.72	500	
Salaries and Wages	1.45	1,000	
Printing and Stationery	7.97	5,500	
Telephone	0.67	460	
			7,460
Net Profit			2,540

Let's look at all the costs involved in the business. This is a nice, easy example because there aren't many, but we can use it to demonstrate the technique. Some of the costs will be **fixed**; that is, they remain the same regardless of sales or production levels.

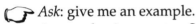 *Ask*: give me an example.

Answer: business rates. Some salaries and wages (possibly all). In fact, it is possible that some of each of the operating costs would be fixed, since a certain amount might be spent on printing and stationery and telephone costs even if there are no sales. Some costs will be **variable**; that is, they will change in direct proportion to the level of sales.

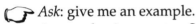 *Ask*: give me an example.

Answer: cost of sales. In fact, this is likely to be the most variable cost of all. Also, that part of each operating expense that is not fixed. Of course, some operating costs will, in fact, be **semi-variable** that is, they will increase as sales increase, but not in direct proportion. In order to demonstrate the technique we will assume in our example that all costs are either fixed or variable.

Before we start, I should point out that the value of the technique depends largely on the accuracy with which we can determine which costs are fixed and which are variable. It therefore follows that the manager will probably be in the best position to identify the fixed and variable costs. For now, we will pretend we are the manager of this business and that we have a clear understanding of how much of our costs are fixed and how much are variable. Given this premise, let's list every cost, dividing each one into its fixed and variable components.

Note: allow the group to determine how much of each cost comes under each section. It does not matter what their allocations are and there will probably be some disagreement, so step in and give arbitrary decisions as expedient. Adopt the same layout as in the prepared example which follows shortly and which you will use afterwards (although the figures will obviously be different). Write their list on the flip-chart and then add the total fixed and variable costs separately.

☞ *Ask*: what percentage do the total variable costs represent to sales?
Note: agree and write the answer in *red* as a percentage next to the total figure for variable costs; circle this and circle the **total** figure for fixed costs (the absolute total, not a percentage) both in *red*.

Now, we have used the information to arrive at two figures which are important to us. One is the total fixed cost; the other is the total variable costs **as a percentage of sales**.

☞ *Ask*: why have we put the total variable costs as a percentage?
Answer: (there may be a pause) because the variable costs will change as the level of sales changes; fixed costs will remain the same in absolute terms. This means that we will be able to calculate the variable costs at any given level of sales from the percentage figure; we also know what the fixed costs will be since they remain the same – within a certain range of increase in activity, at least.

We have come up with our own division between fixed and variable costs; now we will see how the manager in our working example may have allocated the costs.

	Variable	*Fixed*
Cost of Sales	59,000	
Business Rates		500
Salaries and Wages	200	800
Printing and Stationery	1,500	4,000
Telephone	160	300
	60,860	
Important Figure	88.2%	5,600

There is a formula which uses this information to calculate the break-even point. As usual, it is helpful to think through the logic rather than merely pick the formula and use it. The logic goes like this (write each word on the flip-chart as you go):

Sales

Ask: what is sales made up of?
Answer: (there may be another pause!) fixed costs and variable costs.

 Sales (S) = Fixed Costs (FC) + Variable Costs (VC)

Ask: what else?
Answer: net profit. Yes – or net loss.

 Sales (S) = Fixed Costs (FC) + Variable Costs (VC)
+ Net Profit (NP)

Ask: is there anything else which makes up sales?
Answer: no.
Ask: are you *sure*?
Answer: yes! Logically, since *all* costs are either variable or fixed in our example, the only other possible constituent of sales is net profit. If fixed and variable costs exceed sales, we would be left with a minus figure for a net loss. So the formula which includes all the elements which make up sales, logically, must be:

 S = FC + VC + NP

Ask: what is our net profit at the break-even point?
Answer: zero! Therefore, our formula becomes even simpler (at this point, put a large cross over 'NP' and re-write the formula on the next line):

 S = FC + VC

Note: pause and ensure everyone agrees and understands what you have done – they will probably appreciate the time to take notes at this stage as well.

So, in essence, our break-even formula is a very simple relationship between three items; provided we know any two of the items, we can calculate the third. Let's take the figures in our working example. We are going to work out the break-even point.

Ask: what *is* a break-even point?
Answer: the point at which we make neither a profit nor loss. That's net profit or net loss. Okay; in this case, we can't use the sales figure from the Trading, Profit and Loss Account.

👉 *Ask*: why not?
Answer: because we're making a net profit. So:

✍️   S =

We do know the value of our total fixed costs, however:

✍️   S = 5,600 +

👉 *Ask*: what are our variable costs?
Answer: 88.2 per cent *of sales* (not 60,860 – this figure changes as soon as we alter the sales level, which we will be doing if we are selling at the break-even point):

✍️   S = 5,600 + (S × 88.2%)

We can now take the variable cost percentage across to the other side of the formula, reversing its sign, so that we can deal on a like-with-like basis on that side of the equation:

✍️   S – (S × 88.2%) = 5,600

In other words, if we deduct our variable costs (which are 88.2 per cent of sales) from sales we will be left with £5,600 at the break-even point. Now, if all of sales is 100 per cent and we deduct 88.2 per cent, we are left with:

✍️   S × 11.8% = 5,600

👉 *Ask*: what is our break-even point (they will have trouble with this, so allow plenty of time and wait until several people have got the answer before agreeing it!)?

✍️ *Answer*: $\dfrac{5,600}{11.8} \times 100 = 47,458$

In other words, we will break even when we make exactly £47,458 of sales.

👉 *Ask*: how can we check this?
Answer: use that figure and work backwards. I'll demonstrate:

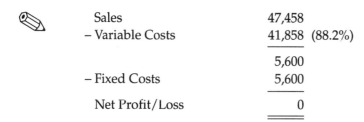

Sales	47,458	
– Variable Costs	41,858	(88.2%)
	5,600	
– Fixed Costs	5,600	
Net Profit/Loss	0	

So we *know* we've done it right! Always check backwards to make sure, as we have done here.

☞ *Ask*: suppose we want to know what level of sales we require in order to make a net profit of, say, £10,000; how can we work this out?
Answer: simple – just add back 'NP' to our formula:

$$S = FC + VC + NP$$

therefore, $S = 5,600 + (S \times 88.2\%) + 10,000$

so, $S - (S \times 88.2\%) = 5,600 + 10,000$

and $S \times 11.8\% = 15,600$

thus $\dfrac{15,600}{11.8} \times 100 = 132,203$

We would therefore need to achieve sales of £132,203 to produce a net profit of £10,000. And now for the proof:

Sales	132,203	
– Variable Costs	116,603	(88.2%)
	15,600	
– Fixed Costs	5,600	
Net Profit/Loss	10,000	

You can see that the break-even formula is extremely useful. It will help you answer any number of questions relating to the levels of sales and net profit at various points. If you alter the fixed costs or the variable cost percentage, you will also be able to calculate the effects these would have.

We can now use this information to construct a break-even chart. This is fairly simple to construct. In fact, it takes the format of a graph. We will draw it following these steps, using the figures from our working example:

1 The vertical axis will measure sales and costs; the horizontal line also measures sales. One common problem is knowing what scale to use. In our example, we have calculated the break-even point as occurring at a level of sales of £47,458. Each axis should be approximately two to three times higher, so that we can see what happens with sales well above the break-even level. If we had a particular sales level planned, we would obviously ensure that the scale of the graph goes at least a little higher than that level.

2 Draw a line representing fixed costs; this will run parallel to the horizontal axis (show Fig 7.1):

3 Plot at least three points on the graph to represent the total cost line. To do this, multiply a given level of sales by the variable cost percentage, add this to the fixed cost and plot the resulting total on the graph. There will be no variable costs when sales are 0, but fixed costs will still occur; the total cost line will therefore start on the vertical axis at the same point that the fixed cost line meets it (show Fig 7.2):

Note: emphasise very strongly that people should not simply plot one point and draw a line between it and the point on the vertical axis where the fixed cost line starts. In any group of trainees, even after giving this warning, some people will still do this. It is almost certain that one of these people will miscalculate their total cost point or start the line at the wrong point on the vertical axis, resulting in a chart that ends up totally wrong. If three points are correctly plotted (and don't let them use the break-even point as one of these.) they should join up and the line should hit the vertical axis at the correct point.

4 The final line to draw is the sales (or revenue) line. A gain, plot three points on the graph where sales measured against the horizontal axis equals sales measured against the vertical axis and draw a line. This line should go through the origin (0). Once more, it is very important not to get lazy. Plot three points without using the origin or the break-even point (show Fig 7.3):

We have now constructed a break-even chart. We can see that the break-even point will be where total costs exactly equal total sales. This is close to the £47,458 sales level which we calculated earlier. However, the graph is on such a large scale that it is impossible to measure the break-even point accurately, no matter how carefully we have drawn it. In order to improve the usefulness of this chart, we can construct it in a different way to reduce the scale. If we leave out cost of sales from variable (and therefore total) costs we will make the figures smaller on the graph (and therefore able to be read off more accurately). At the same time, however, we must exclude cost of sales from the

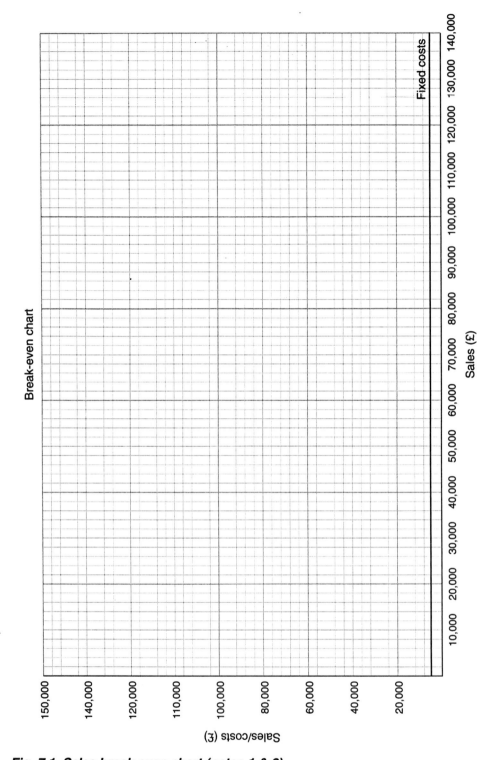

Fig. 7.1 Sales break-even chart (notes 1 & 2)

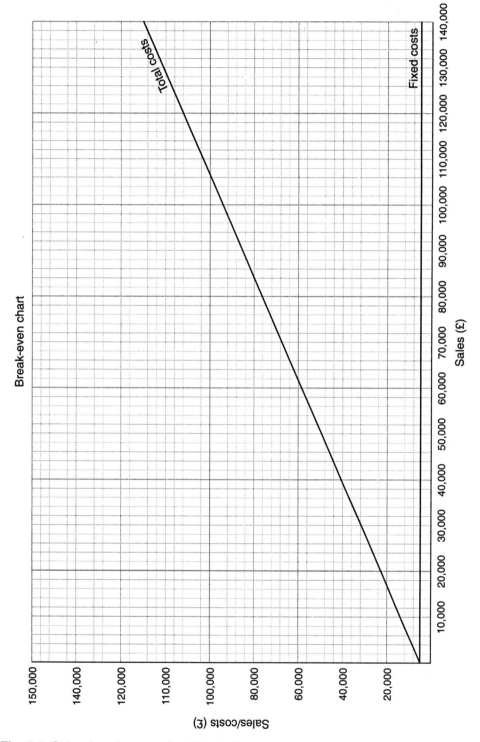

Fig. 7.2 Sales break-even chart (note 3)

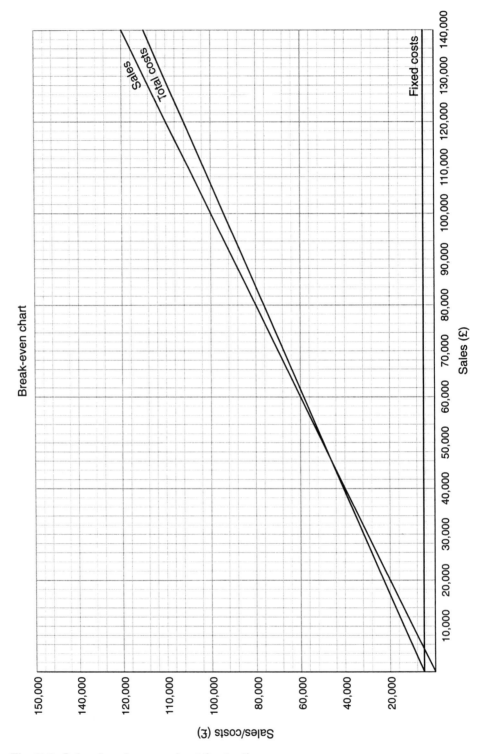

Fig. 7.3 Sales break-even chart (note 4)

other side of the equation; in other words, we will plot gross profit instead of sales against total operating costs. Let's first look at how our arithmetic calculations at the break-even point would now be:

> Gross Profit (GP) = Fixed Operating *Costs* (FOC)
> + Variable Operating Costs (VOC)

Note: let this sink in and make sure that everyone understands what you have done (which is simply to exclude cost of sales from each side of the equation).

Now, using the same figures as before, we can re-work our earlier calculations (but note that we will still end up with the same break-even point, because none of the underlying relationships have changed):

> 14.492753% of Sales = 5,600 + (2.6956521% of Sales)

Note that I have used all the decimal places (which is simple to do when using the memory function of a calculator) in order to prevent the effects of rounding up or down from throwing out our answer.

Ask: what does 14.492753% of sales represent?
Answer: gross profit (we are clarifying *what* it is, not the amount. The percentage is the same as the one from the Trading, Profit and Loss Account but without being rounded.)

5,600 represents the fixed operating costs and remains the same as before (cost of sales, which have now been excluded from our calculations, are all variable). If we add up the variable operating costs, they represent 2.6956521 per cent of sales according to our break-down between fixed and variable costs based on our Trading Profit and Loss Account (check that everyone follows and agrees this).

Without knowing our level of sales at the break-even point (which is what we are trying to establish) we cannot take a percentage away from an absolute figure on the cost side of our formula. What we can do, however, is to transfer the percentage figure to the other side, changing it to a negative value in the process:

> 14.492753 – 2.6956521 (% of Sales) = 5,600

We are now using like with like and can reduce the formula to:

> 11.797101% of Sales = 5,600

Ask: so, what will our sales be at the break-even point?

Answer: 47,469; effectively, the same as before (the slight difference is due to the fact that we did round our variable cost percentage figure in the original example).

It may help to consider a more detailed break-down of the relationships involved based on a chart which I drew up for you several sessions ago.

Break-even formulae

S = Sales
FC = Fixed Costs
VOC = Variable Operating Costs
COS = Cost of Sales
NP = Net Profit
GP = Gross Profit
TVC = Total Variable Costs

At break-even point:

Either $S = FC + VOC + COS$

or $S = FC + TVC$ (*Note*: TVC = COS + VOC)

or $GP = FC + VOC$

At any other point, simply add NP to the right-hand side of whichever formula you are using.

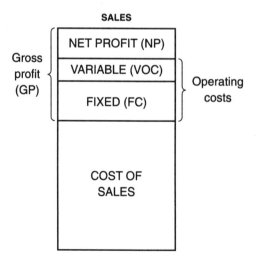

Fig. 7.4 Margin and Mark-up

Remember variable costs are made up of variable operating (or overhead) costs *and* cost of sales. If you use gross profit instead of sales in the formula, then you have already excluded the cost of sales and now only need take account of the variable operating costs. Where you use sales then cost of sales (which are variable) must be added to the variable operating costs in the formula to produce total variable costs. Ultimately, whichever way you do it, total variable costs (including cost of sales) must be taken into account in order to calculate anything.

We can now construct our break-even chart on a basis which uses gross profit and operating costs. Always check the basis on which a chart is drawn up by reading the description on the vertical scale (it should be either sales and costs, or gross profit and (operating) costs).

I have drawn a dotted line down from the break-even point to the horizontal axis (where the sales level at the break-even point can be measured). Show Fig 7.5:

☞ *Ask*: what happens if sales reduce?
Answer: the total (operating) cost line will exceed the gross profit line and the gap between the two (measured against the vertical axis) will represent the **net loss**. If sales exceed the break-even point level, the gap will reverse and represent the **net profit** (demonstrate as necessary).

☞ *Ask*: the break-even chart can be very useful – why?
Answer: it shows the relationships between fixed and variable costs and revenue in a pictorial form (and a picture is worth a thousand words!); we can see what would happen to costs and net profit or loss if we were to achieve a *different* level of sales; we can identify our break-even point and calculate our safety margin (the percentage that our expected sales level could fall short by before making a net loss); we can see what would happen if we change our gross profit margin.

☞ *Ask*: what would happen if we changed our gross profit margin to 25 per cent?
Answer: the new gross profit line would move higher and to the left of the total cost line, thus reaching the break-even point earlier and producing a higher net profit at any (higher) level of sales (show Fig 7.6):

☞ *Ask*: what *disadvantages* are there in using break-even charts?
Answer: they assume all relationships are linear (i.e. change in straight lines); they summarise costs (and possibly different products carrying different gross margins) in one chart; they take no account of the elasticity of demand (i.e. increasing the gross margin may necessitate increasing price and demand may fall off drastically); they are based on arbitrary break-downs between

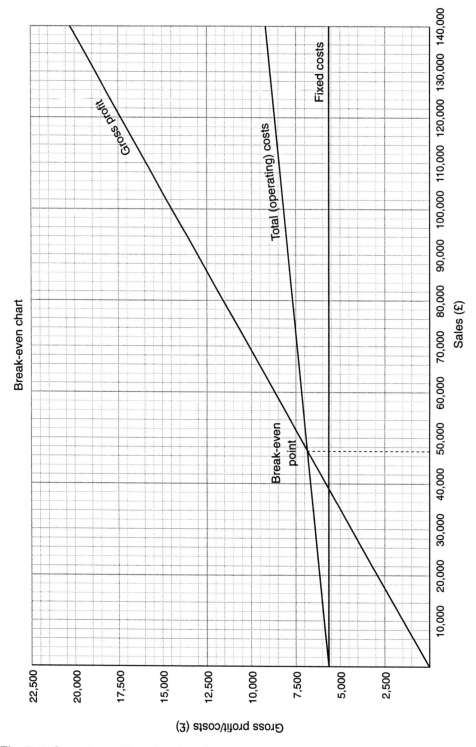

Fig. 7.5 Gross profit break-even chart

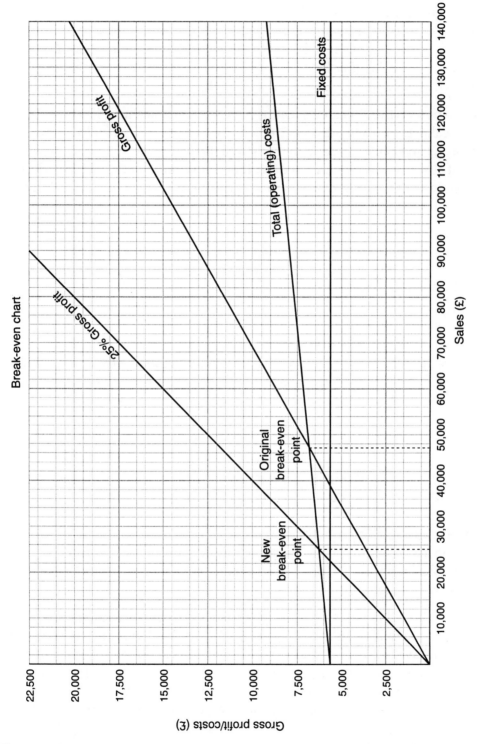

Break-even chart

Gross profit

25% Gross profit

Total (operating) costs

Original break-even point

New break-even point

Fixed costs

Sales (£)

Gross profit/costs (£)

22,500
20,000
17,500
15,000
12,500
10,000
7,500
5,000
2,500

10,000 20,000 30,000 40,000 50,000 60,000 70,000 80,000 90,000 100,000 110,000 120,000 130,000 140,000

Fig. 7.6 Enhanced gross profit break-even chart

fixed and variable costs, either on past performance or *estimated* future fig-ures; they take no account of the capital needed to be employed in order to make a given net profit. This last point means that the break-even chart could show us a very healthy-looking net profit, yet our return on capital employed (which is so important) could be very small.

It can be seen that break-even charts have a number of strengths and a number of weaknesses. They are an extremely useful tool in financial planning and analysis and can be used to demonstrate the likely effects if budgets are suc-cessfully implemented. However, they must not be allowed to hide vital considerations such as cash flow and investment returns – use them, but don't forget their limitations.

There is one last use of the division of costs into their fixed and variable ele-ments that you should be aware of. It is an extremely valuable tool in financial decision-making and very simple, in essence. It is known as **contribution** and is simply this:

Sales – (*all*) variable costs

The resulting figure equals the **contribution** towards the fixed costs and any net profit from sales revenue after all the variable costs have been taken off. Let's look at an example to see why contribution is so significant:

Product	Revenue	Fixed Costs	Variable Costs	Net Profit
X	60,000	15,000	35,000	10,000
Y	10,000	2,500	8,000	(500)
Z	30,000	7,500	20,000	2,500

Fixed costs (totalling £25,000) in this instance have been allocated to the prod-ucts in accordance with their relative sales volume. Under normal profit and loss calculations, it is clear that we should stop selling product Y, since it is making a net loss.

Ask: what will happen if we decide to delete product Y from our range? *Answer:* we will be worse off, since fixed costs (by definition) remain fixed – they will not go away simply because we have cut out one product line. The £25,000 will now therefore be split fully between the remaining two products, thus reducing their net profit. If we look again at product Y, we can see that while producing a net *loss* it is making a **positive contribution** towards the fixed costs (i.e. 10,000 – 8,000). We are, therefore, £2,000 worse off by doing away with product Y.

Perhaps you can now see why some apparently loss-making products, factories, shops and so on are still sold or kept open. Contribution is more important than net profit, unless we can redeploy the resources released to produce a higher contribution with an alternate product, factory or shop.

I will now summarise what we have covered in this chapter:

- the break-even point is reached when income exactly **matches** costs

- costs can be divided into fixed and variable elements

- the variable cost **percentage** is all-important

- for fixed costs, the **absolute** figure is required

- we can **calculate** the level of sales required to break even
- we can also calculate the level of sales needed to achieve a given net profit *or* the net profit or loss which may be expected at a given level of sales.

- a break-even chart can be constructed to illustrate the underlying relationships

- when drawing total cost and gross profit lines, plot **three** points **apart from** the break-even point and the point where the line should intersect with the vertical axis

- the use of break-even charts has many advantages and disadvantages

- *never* lose sight of the importance of cash flow and don't forget about capital employed which is required in order to achieve a given return

- an analysis of *Contribution* can be a very valuable tool in financial decision making

- a positive contribution is often more important than Net Profit

Note: in the following exercises, trainees are expected not to round up or down when using percentages (unless so directed); if they use rounding, their answers will differ slightly from those provided here.

BREAK-EVEN

Exercise M – Question

Using the Trading, Profit and Loss Account from Exercise J, calculate:

1 The anticipated break-even point and prove it.

2 The safety margin by which budgeted sales could fall short before incurring a net loss (in this instance, as a percentage rounded to one decimal place).

3 The level of sales which would be needed to produce a net profit of £20,000 (and prove it).

4 Draw up a break-even chart showing operating costs, gross profit and net profit/loss relationships.

Assume that fixed costs are £50,000 and that the remaining operating costs are variable.

BREAK-EVEN

Exercise M – Answer

1 break-even point

GP = FC + VOC

46.550015% of Sales = 50,000 + (10.12586% of Sales)

46.550015 – 10.12586 (% of Sales) = 50,000

36.424155% of Sales = 50,000

Therefore, **Sales at Break-even** = *£137,272*

Proof:

Sales	137,272
Less, Cost of Sales	73,372
Gross Profit	63,900
Less, Variable Operating Costs	13,900
	50,000
Less, Fixed Costs	50,000
Net Profit	0

2 safety margin

Budgeted Sales	228,030
Break-even Point	137,272
	90,758 **(39.8% of budgeted sales)**

3 sales necessary to achieve a Net Profit of £20,000

GP = FC + VOC + NP

46.550015% of Sales = 50,000 + (10.12586% of Sales) + 20,000

36.424155% of Sales = 50,000 + 20,000

Therefore, Sales required to achieve a Net Profit of £20,000
= **£192,180**

Proof:

Sales	192,180
Less, Cost of Sales	102,720
Gross Profit	89,460
Less, Variable Operating Costs	19,460
	70,000
Less, Fixed Costs	50,000
Net Profit	20,000

Notes

1 The gross profit is calculated as a constant percentage based on the budgeted Trading, Profit and Loss Account figures:

$$\frac{106,148}{228,030} \times 100 = 46.550015\%$$

2 Variable operational costs are calculated in the same way:

$$\frac{73,090 - 50.000}{228,030} \times 100 = 10.12586$$

3 The cost of sales as a percentage is also calculated from the budgeted figures:

$$\frac{121,882}{228,030} \times 100 = 53.449984\%$$

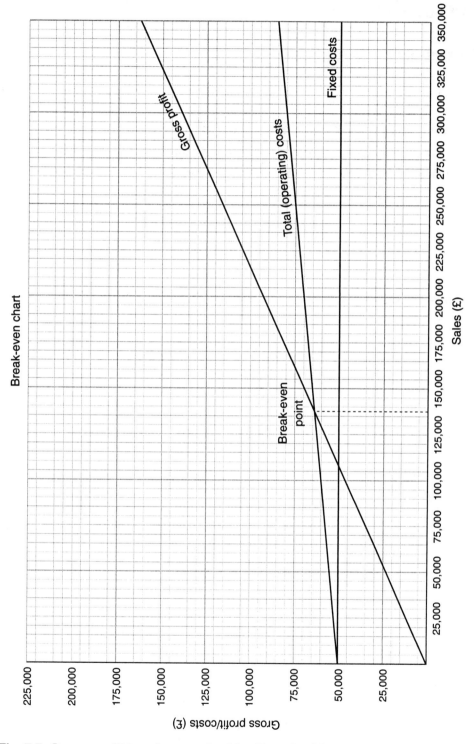

Fig. 7.7 Gross profit break-even chart for Exercise M

BREAK-EVEN

Exercise N – Question

Using the Trading Profit and Loss Account from Exercise K, calculate:

1 The anticipated break-even point and prove it.

2 The safety margin by which budgeted sales could fall short before incurring a net loss (in this instance, as a percentage rounded to one decimal place.

3 The level of sales which would be needed to produce a net profit of £60,000 (and prove it).

4 Draw up a break-even chart showing operating costs, gross profit and net profit/loss relationships.

Assume that variable operating costs are 6 per cent of sales and that the remaining operating costs are fixed

BREAK-EVEN

Exercise N – Answer

1 break-even point

GP = FC + VOC

50% of Sales = 122,580 + (6% of Sales)

50 – 6 (% of Sales) = 122,580

44% of Sales = 122,580

Therefore, **Sales at Break-even = £278,591**

Proof:

Sales	278,591
Less, Cost of Sales	139,296
Gross Profit	139,295
Less, Variable Operating Costs	16,715
	122,580
Less, Fixed Costs	122,580
Net Profit	0

2 safety margin

Budgeted Sales	500,000
Break-even Point	278,591
	221,409 **(44.3% of budgeted sales)**

3 sales necessary to achieve a Net Profit of £60,000

GP = FC + VOC + NP

50% of Sales = 122,580 + (6% of Sales) + 60,000

44% of Sales = 122,580 + 60,000

Therefore, Sales required to achieve a net profit of £60,000
= **£414,955**

Proof:

Sales	414,955
Less, Cost of Sales	207,478
Gross Profit	207,477
Less, Variable Operating Costs	24,897
	182,580
Less, Fixed Costs	122,580
Net Profit	60,000

Notes

Fixed costs (which remain fixed) can be calculated from the budgeted Trading, Profit and Loss Account figures.

Variable operating costs are $\quad$ $500,000 \times 6\% = 30,000$

Therefore, fixed costs must be $\quad$ $152,580 - 30,000 = 122,580$

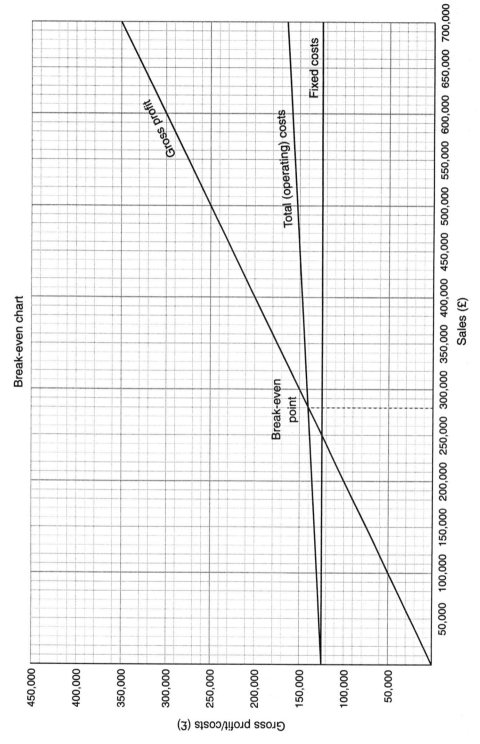

Fig. 7.8 Gross profit break-even chart for Exercise N

REQUIRED SALES LEVEL

Exercise O – Question

What level of sales would be needed to achieve a net profit of £28,450 when working with a gross profit margin of 9.23 per cent, fixed costs of £34,325 and other variable costs running at £17,899 for a sales level of £350,960?

REQUIRED SALES LEVEL

Exercise O – Answer

GP = FC + NP + VOC

9.23% of Sales = £34,325 + £28,450 + (5.10001% of Sales)

9.23 – 5.10001 (% of Sales) = £62,775

4.12999% of Sales = £62,775

Thus, **sales of £1,519,979.40** would be needed in order to achieve a net profit of £28,450.

Proof:

Sales		1,519,979.40
Less,	Cost of Sales	1,379.685.40
	Gross Profit	140,294.10
Less,	Variable Operating Costs	77,519.10
		62,775.00
Less,	Fixed Costs	34,325.00
	Net Profit	28,450.00

EXPECTED NET PROFIT

Exercise P – Question

What net profit would we earn at a level of sales of £48 million, when our gross profit on sales of £2.2 million would be £272,800, with fixed costs then of 5.5 per cent and variable costs equalling £138,600?

EXPECTED NET PROFIT

Exercise P – Answer

Gross Profit as a percentage:

$$\frac{272,800}{2,200,000} \times 100 = 12.4\%$$

Fixed Costs:

$$2,200,000 \times 5.5\% = 121,000$$

Variable Operating Costs:

$$\frac{138,600}{2,200,000} \times 100 = 6.3\%$$

Net Profit at a sales level of £48m:

GP = FC + VOC + NP

£48,000,000 × 12.4% = £121,000 + NP + (6.3% x Sales)

(12.4 – 6.3)% × £48,000,000 = £121,000 + NP

6.1% × £48,000,000 = £121,000 + NP

£2,928,000 = £121,000 + NP

Thus, we would earn a **net profit of £2,807,000** with a sales level of £48m.

Proof:

	Sales	48,000,000
Less,	Cost of Sales	42,048,000
	Gross Profit	5,952,000
Less,	Variable Operating Costs	3,024,000
		2,928,000
Less,	Fixed Costs	121,000
	Net Profit	2,807,000

EXPECTED SALES, FIXED COSTS, NET PROFIT AND CONTRIBUTION

Exercise Q – Question

1 What level of sales would I need to achieve a net profit of £4,250 if the gross profit margin is 28 per cent, fixed costs are £750 and variable costs 5 per cent?

2 If net profit earned is 3.15 per cent of sales, sales are £350,000 and total variable costs are 83.75 per cent of sales, what are the fixed costs?

3 If I increase my sales in (2) above to a level of £425,000, what will my new net profit be?

4 What is the contribution in (3) above?

5 Cost of sales are £35,000; fixed costs are £12,100; net profit on the sales volume of £67,240 is £11,580. What will my net profit be on a sales level of £85,000?

6 What level of sales is required to produce a net profit of £25,000 when, given a sales level of £102,000, variable operating costs are £6,250 and fixed costs are 5 per cent of sales? Opening stock was £12,550, closing stock was £10,000 and the stock turned over every 73 days.

7 In (6) above, what would the net profit be at the sales level of £102,000?

EXPECTED SALES, FIXED COSTS, NET PROFIT AND CONTRIBUTION

Exercise Q – Answer

1 GP = FC + VOC + NP
28% of Sales = 750 + (5% of Sales) + 4,250
28 − 5 (% of Sales) = 750 + 4,250
23% of Sales = 5,000
$$\text{Sales} = \frac{5,000}{23} \times 100$$
Sales = £21,739.13

2 S = FC + TVC + NP
350,000 = FC + (83.75% of Sales) + (3.15% of Sales)
350,000 = FC + (86.9% of Sales)
350,000 × 13.1% = FC
FC = £45,850

3 425,000 = 45,850 + (83.75% of Sales) + NP
425,000 × 16.25% = 45,850 + NP
69,062.50 = 45,850 + NP
NP = £23,212.50

4 £69,062.50

5 Position with sales level of £67,240:

S = FC + VOC + COS + NP
67,240 = 12,100 + VOC + 35,000 + 11,580
67,240 = 58,680 + VOC
VOC = 8,560

Variable operating costs as a percentage:

$$\frac{8,560}{67,240} \times 100 = 12.730517\%$$

Cost of sales as a percentage:

$$\frac{35,000}{67,240} \times 100 = 52.052349\%$$

Total Variable Costs as a percentage:

12.730517% + 52.052349% = 64.782866%

At a new sales level of £85,000:

85,000 = 12,100 + (64.782866% of Sales) + NP
85,000 × 35.21714% = 12,100 + NP
29,934.57 = 12,100 + NP
NP = £17,834.57

6 Cost of sales:

$$\text{average stock} = \frac{12,550 + 10,000}{2}$$

average stock = 11,275

stock turns over every 73 days, or $\dfrac{365}{73}$ = 5 times per year

COS = 11,275 × 5 = 56,375

Total variable costs:

TVC = COS + VOC
TVC (at a sales level of 102,000) = 56,375 + 6,250
TVC = 62,625

Total variable costs as a percentage:

$$\frac{62,625}{102,000} \times 100 = 61.397058\%$$

Fixed costs:

102,000 x 5% = 5,100

Sales level required to produce a net profit of £25,000:

S = FC + TVC + NP
S = 5,100 + (61.397058% of Sales) + 25,000
S = 30,100 + (61.397058% of Sales)
S x 38.60295% = 30,100

$$\frac{30,100}{38.60295} \times 100 = S$$

S = £77,973.31

7 $102,000 = 5,100 + (61.397058\% \text{ of Sales}) + NP$
$102,000 \times 38.60295\% = 5,100 + NP$
$39,375.01 = 5,100 + NP$
NP = £34,275.01

CONTRIBUTION ANALYSIS IN DECISION MAKING

Exercise R – Question

A company has five branches which produce the following performance figures:

Branch	Sales	Gross Profit Margin	Branch Operating Costs
1	250,000	26%	52,500
2	300,000	20%	65,000
3	200,000	24%	60,000
4	750,000	22%	115,000
5	500,000	30%	80,000

The head office incurs costs of £100,000, which are allocated to the five branches in proportion to their turnover and included in the branch operating costs; all sales are made through the branches. Assess the situation of the company and make recommendations for any changes which might be beneficial, showing the overall effects of any changes you make.

CONTRIBUTION ANALYSIS IN DECISION MAKING

Exercise R – Answer

Current situation

Branch	Sales	Gross Profit	Variable Costs	Contribution
1	250,000	65,000	40,000	25,000
2	300,000	60,000	50,000	10,000
3	200,000	48,000	50,000	(2,000)
4	750,000	165,000	77,500	87,500
5	500,000	150,000	55,000	95,000
Total	2,000,000	488,000	272,500	215,500
Fixed Costs				100,000
Net Profit				115,500

£115,000 is 5.77% of sales.

Suggested change

Branch 3 is making a **negative** contribution. In effect, this means it is adding to the fixed costs! It would be better to close it down. If we do this, the total contribution from the remaining branches will increase to £217,500. Fixed costs (the head office costs) remain the same (although allocated differently) and so the new net profit for the company will be £117,500. As a percentage of the new sales figure, net profit is 6.53 per cent. We need to work less hard to increase our overall return!

Note

If we had allocated the head office cost (in effect, the fixed costs!) to each branch in proportion to its turnover, branch 2 would produce a net loss of £5,000:

Sales – Fixed Cost – Variable Costs = Net Profit
300,000 – 15,000 – 290,000 = (5,000)

All branch costs *except* the share of head office expenses (which remain if the branch is closed) are, in effect, variable. In our original table, branch costs were £65,000; deduct the head office costs of £15,000 (15% of £100,000) from this figure and add the cost of sales (80% of £300,000) to give the total variable costs for this branch (£290,000). We now arrive at a net loss for the branch. However, it is making a positive **contribution** of £5,000 which would be lost if the branch was closed. Contribution analysis tells us we should not close branch 2, but we should close branch 3.

IMPORTANT FORMULAE

Exercise S – Question

Without reference to your notes, write out the correct formulae (or procedure where marked *) which would normally produce the following information:

1* To convert a percentage to a fraction
2* To convert a fraction to a percentage
3 Mark-up
4* To convert a mark-up to a margin
5* To convert a margin to a mark-up
6 Cost of goods sold (there are at least two ways of calculating this figure)
7 Gross profit margin
8 Net profit margin
9 Net capital employed
10 Return on net capital employed (as a percentage)
11 Rate of stock turnover
12 Rate of debtor turnover
13 Rate of creditor turnover
14 Number of months stock is held on average
15 Number of days stock is held on average
16 Number of months credit is extended on average
17 Number of days credit is extended on average
18 Number of months credit is received on average
19 Number of days credit is received on average
20 Write three formulae which show the relationships between capital, assets and liabilities
21 Working capital
22 Net assets
23 Current ratio
24 Liquid ratio
25 Sales required to produce a given level of net profit
26 Sales at break-even point
27 Contribution
28 Ratio of ownership interest to total claims on an organisation
29 Gearing ratio
30 Yield
31 EPS
32 P/E Ratio

IMPORTANT FORMULAE

Exercise S – Answer

1 Percentage to fraction: Place the percentage over 100. To reduce, divide by the highest common denominator

2 Fraction to percentage: Divide the top figure by the bottom figure and multiply the answer by 100

3 Mark-up

$$= \frac{\text{Gross Profit}}{\text{Cost of Sales}} \times 100$$

4 Mark-up to margin: Convert percentage to a fraction; the top figure remains the same but is added to the bottom figure to get the new bottom figure. Convert the resulting fraction back to a percentage

5 Margin to mark-up: Convert percentage to a fraction; the top figure remains the same but is subtracted from the bottom figure to get the new bottom figure. Convert the resulting fraction back to a percentage.

6 Cost of goods sold
or,

$= $ Opening Stock + Purchases – Closing Stock
$= $ Stockturn $\times$ Average Stock at Cost Price

7 Gross profit margin

$$= \frac{\text{Gross Profit}}{\text{Sales}} \times 100$$

8 Net profit margin

$$= \frac{\text{Net Profit}}{\text{Sales}} \times 100$$

9 Net capital employed

$= $ Fixed Assets + Current Assets – Current Liabilities (possibly excluding bank overdraft)

10 % Return on net capital employed

$$= \frac{\text{Net Profit before Tax}}{\text{Net Capital Employed}} \times 100$$

11 Rate of stock turnover $= \dfrac{\text{Cost of Sales}}{\text{Average Stock at Cost price}}$

12 Rate of debtor turnover $= \dfrac{\text{Sales}}{\text{Average Debtors}}$

13 Rate of creditor turnover $= \dfrac{\text{Purchases}}{\text{Average Creditors}}$

14 Average number of months stock is held $= \dfrac{12}{\text{Rate of Stock Turnover}}$

15 Average number of days stock is held $= \dfrac{365}{\text{Rate of Stock Turnover}}$

16 Number of months credit is extended on average $= \dfrac{12}{\text{Rate of Debtor Turnover}}$

17 Number of days credit is extended on average $= \dfrac{365}{\text{Rate of Debtor Turnover}}$

18 Number of months credit is received on average $= \dfrac{12}{\text{Rate of Creditor Turnover}}$

19 Number of days credit is received on average $= \dfrac{365}{\text{Rate of Creditor Turnover}}$

20 Capital = Assets − Liabilities
Capital + Liabilities = Assets
Assets − Capital = Liabilities

21 Working Capital = Current Assets − Current Liabilities

22 Net Assets = Total Assets − Current Liabilities

23 Current Ratio $= \dfrac{\text{Current Assets}}{\text{Current Liabilities}}$

24 Liquid Ratio $= \dfrac{\text{Debtors + Cash}}{\text{Current Liabilities}}$
(possibly excluding bank overdraft)

25 Sales = Fixed Costs + Variable Costs + Net Profit
or, Sales − Variable Costs = Fixed Costs + Net Profit

26 Sales at Break-even Point:
Fixed costs = Sales − Variable Costs
or
(Gross Margin as % − Variable Costs as %) × (Sales) = Fixed Costs

27 Contribution = Sales − Variable Costs

28 Ratio of ownership interest to total claims $= \dfrac{\text{Capital} + \text{Profit} + \text{Reserves}}{\text{Capital} + \text{Profit} + \text{Reserves} + \text{Liabilities}}$

29 Gearing ratio $= \dfrac{\text{Fixed Interest Capital}}{\text{Total Capital}}$

Alternative gearing ratio $= \dfrac{\text{Fixed Interest Capital}}{\text{Owners' Capital}}$

30 Yield $= \dfrac{\text{Dividend}}{\text{Share Price}} \times 100$

31 EPS $= \dfrac{\text{Net Profit}}{\text{Number of Shares}}$

32 P/E ratio $= \dfrac{\text{Share Price}}{\text{EPS}}$

A final note for the person using this book

Conducting training sessions on such a technical subject can be interesting but daunting; accountants aren't usually trainers, or trainers accountants! I have tried to write the material in such a way that a skilful trainer will be able to conduct a complete training course if required. However, help is available if you feel that the material is right but your confidence and technical knowledge is still insufficient to conduct your own training course on this subject. If you would like me to conduct an in-house three-day Finance for Non-Financial Managers course or send people on an external course, please contact me:

Derrick Fellows,
Consultancy and Training Services,
63, Wynndale Road,
Woodford,
London, E18 1DY,
United Kingdom.

Telephone: 0181-504 4639

READY MADE ACTIVITIES
RESOURCE PACKS

Developing your Staff
Selling Skills
Customer Care Skills
Negotiation Skills
Presentation Skills
Financial Skills

In a high pressure environment you need to bring your team up to speed quickly and effectively. Waiting for the right course can waste time.

The *Ready Made Activities Resource Packs* give you access to material to develop your own skills and those of your staff in vital areas such as finance, negotiation and customer care.

You can see how simple it is to improve the skills of your staff and save your company thousands of pounds by completing the training yourself. It couldn't be easier with our unique new *Ready Made Activities Resource Pack* – and you don't have to be an expert or even have any training experience to use them!.

These special versions of the Ready Made Activities series come with the full endorsement of the Institute of Management and are available in a Ringbound Presentation Folder containing all the information you could need to present the new skills to your team.

All the *Ready Made Activities Resource Packs* come complete with
● Overhead Transparencies – impress your colleagues and your bosses with a professional presentation
● Free Video – reinforce the message or open your sessions with this ice-breaker
● Photocopiable Handouts – give your staff the key points of your presentation to take away and refer to again and again.

All this and more for only £120.00*

Available direct from Pitman Publishing
Telephone 071 379 7383 or fax 071 240 5771

*Price correct at time of going to press but is subject to change without notice